The New Politics

for my mother

The New Politics

*Catholic Social Teaching
for the Twenty-First Century*

edited by Paul Vallely

SCM PRESS

0 334 02748 9

First published 1998
by SCM Press
9–17 St Albans Place, London N1 0NX

SCM Press is a division of
SCM-Canterbury Press Ltd

Typeset by Regent Typesetting, London
and printed in Great Britain by
Biddles Ltd, Guildford and King's Lynn

Contents

Acknowledgments

This book is based on a series of lectures given at the church of St Margaret of Scotland, in East Twickenham, in memory of the former parish priest, the late Canon Desmond Swan, in the hope that the torch of social justice which burned so fiercely in his mild hand might be passed on to his successor. Those who knew him give thanks for Desmond and all he did and was. Thanks, too, to Sister Colette of the Franciscan Missionaries of Our Lady and Fr Patrick Fitzgerald of the Missionaries of Africa (White Fathers), whose dedicated work in Ethiopia and Zambia has been an inspiration to the parishioners of St Margaret's for more than a decade.

My thanks to the lecturers for their co-operation and their patience with me in the process of turning their texts into the chapters of this book which I fear was more demanding than they had anticipated. I am grateful to Julie Clague, Julian Filochowski and Clifford Longley for their guidance on sections of the manuscript other than their own. And particular thanks to Christine Morgan who picked a clear path through the thicket of my ideas on the dialogue between Catholic Social Teaching and secular society in the future.

Bibliography of Principal Texts of Catholic Social Teaching

In the notes the principal documents of Catholic Social Teaching are referred to by the initials which follow below. Editions of the encyclicals vary, hence where a number follows the abbreviation this refers to a paragraph rather than a page number. The encyclicals from *Rerum Novarum* to *Sollicitudo Rei Socialis* are available in a single volume, *Proclaiming Justice and Peace: One Hundred Years of Catholic Social Teaching*, edited by Michael Walsh and Brian Davies, Collins/CAFOD, London 1991. The later texts were each published in English by the Catholic Truth Society, London, in the year indicated.

Rerum Novarum	RN	1891	Leo XIII
Quadragesimo Anno	QA	1931	Pius XI
Mater et Magistra	MM	1961	John XXIII
Pacem in Terris	PT	1963	John XXIII
Gaudium et Spes	GS	1965	Second Vatican Council
Populorum Progressio	PP	1967	Paul VI
Octagesima Adveniens	OA	1971	Paul VI
Justice in the World	JW	1971	The Synod of Bishops
Evangelii Nuntiandi	EN	1975	Paul VI
Redemptor Hominis	RH	1979	John Paul II
Dives in Misericordia	DM	1980	John Paul II
Laborem Exercens	LE	1981	John Paul II
Sollicitudo Rei Socialis	SRS	1987	John Paul II
Centesimus Annus	CA	1991	John Paul II
Tertio Millennio Adveniente	TMA	1994	John Paul II
Evangelium Vitae	EV	1995	John Paul II

Introduction

History ended in 1989 with the fall of the Berlin Wall. Such was the thesis of Francis Fukuyama, the American political historian who saw in the collapse of communism in the Soviet bloc not just the end of an epoch but something far more fundamental. Until that point the history of the twentieth century had been marked by a debate, ideological and martial, between the forces of capitalism and communism. These two opposing empires had offered competing visions on how human society might be ordered. Now one had crumbled and the triumph of the other was to proceed unchecked. Human social and economic development would no longer be governed by a competition or even a dialectic between the two. All we could expect was more of the same – capitalism – perhaps in a form which was more sophisticated, perhaps more brutally unfettered now that politicians and employers felt there was no need to tame the harsher elements of the market system to prevent those it alienated turning to communism. But no significant alternative would emerge.

Fukuyama published his thought in his book *The End of History* and almost all contemporary political thinkers seemed to genuflect to that inevitability. It was easy to agree. In the Far East the ancient philosophies of Buddhism, Hinduism and Confucianism offered no alternative. Rather they seemed to have tempered the societies of the countries we called the Asian Tigers (in homage to the strength and ferocity of their then rocketing economies) and somehow made their capitalism even stronger than ours.

We are all capitalists now, lamented one old socialist. His colleagues on the Left unwillingly concurred. The arguments of the hard Left – that real socialism had never been tried in the Eastern bloc – seemed hopelessly utopian. In the years that followed the Left largely drifted aimlessly. Many people retained the instincts that some mechanism had to be adopted to make that capitalism more compassionate than the red-in-tooth-and-claw variety espoused by the monetarist economists and deregulationists of the Thatcher and Reagan era. This alternative instinct found some release in the concerns of environmentalism and the green movement. Yet these were short-lived or partial. For they focussed on one aspect of modern life only. They lacked comprehensiveness. There seemed no alternative position from which to develop a full critique of capitalism.

And yet such a position did exist. It had been developed over a century of thinking which was convinced that neither the apologias for unbridled capitalism nor the totalitarian rigidity of communism were the only alternatives. For more than a hundred years the Roman Catholic Church has subjected the economic certainties of capitalism and communism to a scrutiny which has slowly developed an entirely new position from which today to survey the capitalist leviathan. The body of analytical tools which it compiled slowly cohered into the philosophical framework which has become known as Catholic Social Teaching. What this book sets out to do is chronicle that development and highlight the insights it has formed which have particular resonance to the world as it enters the twenty-first century – a world in which unprecedented ferocity in global economic competition is predicted of an extent that it will not leave any child, woman or man untouched anywhere across the globe.

That world – the hard reality of it in the present era, and the spectre of a more cruel version in the decades to come – is one which has prompted electorates all over the world to search for some new techniques or philosophies to cushion or mitigate the effects of the new post-historic capitalism. Uniquely Catholic Social Teaching offers insights whose appeal is far from restricted to Catholics or even Christians. In the chapters which follow a series of distinguished commentators spell out the legacy of a century of that evolving thought – laying particular emphasis upon the more recent developments under Pope John Paul II who has written almost as much on social issues as all his predecessors combined. The authors then offer suggestions as to how this thought might shape the formation of a new political era, combining economic efficiency with greater social sensitivity to create a more effective and compassionate society.

There will be those who are surprised to have it said that the church has been developing this philosophical approach over only a century. In a sense they are right for as Michael Walsh, the Librarian at Heythrop College, University of London, spells out in his opening chapter, the church has always had some form of social teaching. The earliest Christian writers concerned themselves with the morality of ownership of property and money and they touched upon the relationship between church and state. The Christian philosophizers of the Middle Ages included in their deliberations questions of economics, enunciating the concepts of a 'just price' and 'fair wage', and pronouncing at length on the question of usury. Yet such thinking was never systematic. It was only at the end of the last century that individual thought about social relationships began to be developed into a coherent system of social teaching.

It was historically conditioned. At the end of the nineteenth century it was becoming increasingly evident to church leaders that there was a down-side to the massive wealth which the Industrial Revolution was creating for the rulers and owners of Europe. The abject living conditions of many ordinary working men and women, and their children, revealed the exploitative underbelly of capitalism. It prompted, too, the rise of communism, and the materialistic atheism which accompanied it. Perhaps just as significantly, argues Walsh, it was only at this point that the pope lost the Papal States during the unification of Italy and ceased to be a temporal ruler who squabbled over territory and power along with all the other monarchs of Europe. Yet whatever the confluence of historical forces at this time the result was the development of a new consciousness within the Vatican which produced a new way of thinking about the world. Since the Emperor Constantine had placed the institutions of Rome at the service of Christianity, and vice versa, the church, despite the lifestyle of its itinerant founder, had almost always instinctively taken the side of authority and the rich. And yet it had also always set its face against individualism and defined Christians as persons living in community. Freed of the burdens of temporal office Leo XIII set about resolving these contradictory elements.

The result was *Rerum Novarum* (1891), the first in what were to prove a series of papal encyclicals on social issues. When this treatise on the rights of the worker was published it caused shock-waves with its condemnation of a situation in which a 'tiny group of extravagantly rich men have been able to lay upon the great multitude of unpropertied workers a yoke little better than that of slavery itself'.[1] The excesses of capitalism were condemned: 'The first task is to save the wretched workers from the brutality of those who make use of human beings as mere instruments for the unrestrained acquisition of profits'.[2] The mediaeval notion of a just wage was restated: 'The wage ought not to be in any way insufficient for the bodily needs of a temperate and well-behaved worker. If having no alternative and fearing a worse fate, a workman is forced to accept harder conditions imposed by an employer or contractor, he is the victim of violence against which justice cries out'.[3] Yet for all the vigour of its language – and the fact that it was condemned as a socialist document at the time – it was essentially a plea to the common sense of the ruling classes: 'The condition of the workers is the question of the hour. It will be answered one way or another, rationally or irrationally, and which way it goes is of the greatest importance to the state.'[4]

The core of the common good

The key fact was this: in the course of his attempt to shame the rich into better behaviour the pope began the process of formulating the set of principles which evolved over the intervening hundred years to point the way to a new politics for the twenty-first century. As

Walsh warns, we must be careful in attempting to draw general conclusions from teachings which were drawn up in response to the needs of the time by popes who may very well all have had their own personal agendas. Nonetheless from out of the turmoil of the times there began to emerge certain core principles. At their heart is the notion of the 'common good' which had its roots in the thinking of the great mediaeval theologian St Thomas Aquinas who synthesized the thought of Aristotle and St Augustine, bringing together the two great traditions of Western culture – the philosophy of the great classical pagan writers with the theology of the early church fathers. There had been hints of the common good in Plato's suggestion that the goal of the state ought to be 'the greatest possible happiness of the city as a whole and not that of any one class'.[5] It was there too in Augustine's idea of 'the advantageousness, the common participation in which makes a people'.[6] Orientation to the common good is laid down by Aquinas as one of the defining features of law;[7] in defending capital punishment – because it subordinates the good of the individual to that of the community – he speaks of occasions when an execution is necessary 'in order to preserve the common good'.[8]

All this goes well beyond the notion of the utilitarian thinkers that the right ordering of society should produce what the Scottish philosopher Francis Hutcheson called that 'which procures the greatest happiness for the greatest numbers'.[9] Certainly it is not the same as Bentham's suggestion that the best interests of the community are synonymous with 'the sum of the interests of the several members who compose it'.[10] It is more than the dictatorship of the majority. It respects the integrity of the individual as well as creating the conditions for human co-operation and the achievement of shared objectives. It contains an almost mystical element which the German ascetic Thomas à Kempis captured when he wrote: 'Never be completely idle, but either reading, or writing, or praying, or meditating, or at some useful work for the common good.'[11] Or as Pope John XXIII was to put it in *Mater et Magistra* (1961), it embraces 'all those social conditions which favour the full development of human personality'.[12] It does away with the old

black and white distinction between selfish action and altruistic
action. We contribute to the common good because we want to live
in a society which is fair and just. If it is fair and just to others
it will be fair and just to us too. We do not have to agonize about
our motives, nor bribe or excuse ourselves with concepts like
enlightened self-interest. The service of the common good is an
end in itself.

This is what was in Leo XIII's mind when he wrote in that first
social encyclical, *Rerum Novarum*: 'the end of civil society is
centred in the common good in which one and all, in due propor-
tion have a right to participate'. He went on:

> The state has one basic purpose for existence, which embraces
> in common the highest and the lowest of its members. Non-
> owning workers are unquestionably citizens by nature in virtue
> of the same right as the rich . . . Since it would be quite absurd
> to look out for one portion of the citizens and to neglect another,
> it follows that public authority ought to exercise due care in safe-
> guarding the well-being and the interests of non-owning work-
> ers. Unless this is done, justice, which commands that everyone
> be given his own, will be violated. Wherefore St Thomas says
> wisely: 'Even as part and whole are in a certain way the same, so
> too that which pertains to the whole pertains in a certain way to
> the part also.'[13]

From it grew a respect for the rights of each individual, a person
made in the image of God:

> Equity therefore commands that public authority show proper
> concern for the worker so that from what he contributes to the
> common good he may receive what will enable him, housed,
> clothed, and secure, to live his life without hardship. Whence, it
> follows that all those measures ought to be favoured which seem
> in any way capable of benefiting the condition of workers. Such
> solicitude is so far from injuring anyone, that it is destined rather
> to benefit all, because it is of absolute interest to the state that

those citizens should not be miserable in every respect from whom such necessary goods proceed.[14]

From this starting point Pope Leo set out the building blocks for the development of the social teaching which was to follow. The creation of wealth through capitalism was endorsed, but with a pointed insistence about how that wealth should be equitably distributed. The primacy of people over things and of labour over capital was established. So was the notion that the market can never be allowed to operate unchecked or without regard for the moral framework in which it must exist. The right of workers to join trade unions was set out, even if Leo XIII did think of them in the mould of mediaeval guilds and assumed they would be exclusively Catholic.

But socialism was given short shrift: 'when socialists endeavour to transfer privately owned goods into common ownership they worsen the condition of all wage-earners. By taking away from them freedom to dispose of their wages they rob them of all hope and opportunity of increasing their possessions and bettering their conditions.'[15] As a result 'all incentives for individuals to exercise their ingenuity and skill would be removed and the very founts of wealth dry up. The dream of equality would become the reality of equal want and degradation for all.'[16] Moreover the Marxist notion that class war would bring about the changes which brought justice to the workers was firmly ruled out; an abhorrence of 'class struggle' has remained an unwavering principle of Catholic Social Teaching ever since.

Leo XIII envisaged, too, an increasing role for the state in resolving class conflict – something which was to gain importance in the thinking of later popes and which has important insights to offer a world in which, for all the more recent talk of the need to diminish the role of the state, it still plays an increasing role in the life of the modern citizen – in the UK the percentage of the national income which is taken in tax is higher today, even despite the rhetoric of the era of Thatcherism, than it has ever been.

The emergence of subsidiarity

It is in this context that the papal concept of subsidiarity – the idea
that the state should not take over what individuals or groups can
do – is a significant development. The popes who followed Leo
XIII – Pius X and Benedict XV – made no significant contribution
to the development of the church's social teaching. Then in 1931
Quadragesimo Anno, was issued by Pope Pius XI on the fortieth
anniversary of *Rerum Novarum*. It is here that the principle of
subsidiarity makes its first appearance, preceded by the admoni-
tion: 'It is gravely wrong to take from individuals what they can
accomplish by their own initiative and industry and give it to the
community.'[17] The notion of subsidiarity asserts that decisions
should be taken at the lowest level possible which is compatible
with good government. This concept is a significant tool in maintaining the rights of the individual or the small community over the
battalions of big government. The state should not do what the
local authority can discharge, a local council should not take to
itself what might be done by smaller local groups or even individuals. And the need for a proper balance between individual
economic freedom and the promotion of common values is hinted
at: 'The right ordering of economic life cannot be left to a free
competition of forces. From this source as from a poisoned
spring have originated and spread all the errors of individualistic
economic teaching.'[18]

   But if the foundations for a century of Catholic Social Teaching
had been laid, the church was still very much turned in on itself.
The pope who followed, Pius XII, (1939–58) did nothing to change
this. It was not until the 1960s that a fundamental shift came which
turned Catholic Social Teaching fully out to the world. The man
who made the difference was the charismatic Pope John XXIII
who imbued the church with a new optimism. His new tone was
that of the 1960s, a time of affluence and celebration of the benefits
of social, political and technical change. His encyclical *Pacem
in Terris* (1963) was the first not to be addressed simply to the
church but to 'all people of good will'. Catholics, he declared, must

cease their separateness and join in public life to bring change from within.

All this was not merely a reflection of the changing times. It was an organic development of previous papal social teaching. John XXIII took the concept of the common good and built upon it:

> The attainment of the common good is the sole reason for the existence of civil authorities[19] . . . For the common good, since it is intimately bound up with human nature, can never exist fully and completely unless the human person is taken into account at all times[20] . . . It is in the nature of the common good that every single citizen has the right to share in it . . . Hence every civil authority must strive to promote the common good in the interests of all, without favouring any individual citizen or category of citizen . . . Nevertheless, considerations of justice and equity can at times demand that those in power pay more attention to the weaker members of society, since these are at a disadvantage when it comes to defending their own rights and asserting their legitimate interests . . .[21]

> The common good is something which affects the needs of the whole individual, body and soul[22] . . . [it] is best safeguarded when personal rights and duties are guaranteed[23] . . . Thus any government which refused to recognize human rights, or acted in violation of them, would not only fail in its duty; its decrees would be wholly lacking in binding force.[24]

The new emphases began the process of breaking the link which previous generations had taken for granted between Roman Catholicism and the forces of social conservatism, says Brian Davies, who was studying theology as a Jesuit at the time, in chapter 2. The common good demanded not equality for the poor but preference; they stood not beside the rich but before them. The words were not yet used but the 'option for the poor' had been formulated. Human rights, which the church had once derided as a flawed secular notion, had become integral to its vision of the

dignity of the human person; made in the image of God each
person has universal and inalienable rights and duties – what helps
the person to grow is good; what inhibits and destroys is bad. It
raises questions in the modern world, argues Davies, a former
Head of Education at the English and Welsh Bishops' official aid
and development agency, CAFOD, about issues such as the rights
of refugees and asylum-seekers and the way governments use
unemployment as a tool to keep inflation down. Individuals have
the right to participate in the decisions which affect their lives. But
the state should also play a more active role in working for the
common good; there may be situations in which social justice takes
priority over economic efficiency and requires the state to nation-
alize firms, so long as the principle of subsidiarity was also
observed. The state may impose controls on major companies to
obtain social justice – a suggestion which Davies considers to be
even more apt with the tendency of the globalization of the world's
economy to increase the sense of disempowerment among individuals and to assume for ideological reasons that the privatization
of nationalized industries in the Third World always brings more
advantages than disadvantages. What was true of individuals also
applied to nations. The common good of the state was but an echo
of a wider common good of humanity. In this every state has the
right to exist and to determine the nature of its own development
– but rich nations have a duty to help poor ones do this, through
aid which does not undermine national integrity – a notion which,
Davies notes, runs counter to the orthodoxy of the neo-liberal free
market solutions imposed on poor nations by the West towards the
end of the twentieth century.

The Second Vatican Council completed the process by which
the church turned to embrace the world:

The joys and the hopes, the griefs and the anxieties of the
people of this age, especially those who are poor or in any way
afflicted, these are the joys and hopes, the griefs and anxieties of
the followers of Christ.[25]

Those were the words which opened the council's document on 'The Church in the Modern World' which eventually was published as *Gaudium et Spes* (1965). It again put social justice at the heart of its vision, insisting on 'everyone's right to affirm their own culture' but pronouncing that 'it cannot be denied that people are often diverted from doing good and spurred towards evil by the social circumstances in which they live and were immersed from their birth'.[26] Underscoring 'the exalted dignity proper to the human person'[27] it proclaimed:

> Therefore, there must be made available to all men and women everything necessary for leading a life truly human, such as food, clothing, and shelter; the right to choose a state of life freely and to found a family; the right to education and employment, to a good reputation, to respect, to appropriate information, to activity in accord with the upright norms of one's own conscience, to protection of privacy and to rightful freedom.[28]

What John XXIII and the Second Vatican Council had done was fundamentally redefine something at the heart of Catholic Social Teaching. More than that they had redefined what was understood by 'church'. The church no longer thought of itself as a 'perfect society' whose focus was inwards to its sacramental life. Instead it had become open to the world, and embarked upon a strategy of 'reading the signs of the times' to discover where God's Spirit was at work in the wider world.

Significantly from this point onwards encyclicals abandoned the old style of reasoning from natural law – the philosophical stance which presumed that God's plan for the world was evident in human nature and could be discerned by applying human reason. From *Rerum Novarum* onwards papal encyclicals had used this method, which was deemed to be accessible by all people, Christian or not; distinctively Christian sources of wisdom were not employed. This changed with Vatican II, where church leaders lamented the gap which existed between faith and everyday life and determined to bridge the two. It was a move from abstract philosophy to historical consciousness, from immutable essences to the changing facts of history, from deduction to induction, from the classical world to one which took account of Freud and Marx, from theory to the real life of ordinary people. From this point there were none of the grand plans for the reconstruction of the social order proposed in *Quadragesimo Anno* by Pius XI. Documents began with a consideration of a particular topic, or a section of the gospel which illuminated such a contemporary reality.

A just economic order

Having embraced the world the church discovered the need to face up to some of the world's inequalities. Where previous encyclicals had been written from an essentially European perspective, *Populorum Progressio* (1967) by the next pope, Paul VI, attempts to be truly catholic. It brought the Third World, for the first time, fully into the considerations of Catholic social justice. Considering the relationship between rich nations it concluded that 'economic justice is essential for peace' and famously proclaimed: 'Development is the new name for peace.'

Populorum Progressio criticized capitalism more strongly than earlier Catholic Social Teaching. The profit motive and the unrestricted use of private property were scrutinized more acutely. And it elaborated what amounted to a definite option in favour of the powerless and oppressed. The document *Justice in the World*, produced by the 1971 Synod of Bishops after its meeting in Rome, spelled out whom the church included as the voiceless victims of injustice – migrants, refugees, political prisoners, landless peasants and others. But what was significant about Paul VI's contribution, argues Julian Filochowski, the director of CAFOD, in chapter 3, was not that he named the victims. Rather he identified the structures which victimized them.

Structural injustice, the bishops of Latin America had pronounced at their seminal conference in Medellín in 1968 which was a crucible of liberation theology, is a form of institutionalized violence. Paul VI responds to this by calling for change in the financial and trading relationship between nations. He also questioned the models of growth and development which the rich northern half of the globe offers, or imposes on, the poor South. Development must involve 'integral human development' – the notion that *everyone* in the poor society must benefit from the process. He expressed concern about the potential for abuse and domination from the uncontrolled power of multinational companies.[29] But his chief concern was for the unfair nature of the relationship itself, which he sees embodied in the very system of so-called 'free' trade:

> It is evident that the principle of free trade, by itself, is no longer adequate for regulating international agreements. It certainly can work when both parties are about equal . . . but the case is quite different when the nations involved are far from equal. Market prices that are freely agreed upon can turn out to be quite unfair. It must be avowed openly that in this case the fundamental tenet of liberalism as it is so called, as the norm for market dealings, is open to serious question . . . When two parties are in very unequal positions, their mutual consent does not alone guarantee a fair contract; the rule of free consent remains subservient to the demands of the natural law.[30]

The rule of free trade, taken by itself, he concluded, 'is no longer able to govern international relations'. It can be called just only when it conforms to the demands of social justice. It must therefore always be subordinated to the principle that the earth and all it produces are intended for the benefit of all. This is a doctrine which bears renewed scrutiny in the globalized economy of the twenty-first century when – through the strictures of the structural adjustment packages imposed upon the Third World by the International Monetary Fund and World Bank – poor nations are required in the name of free trade to lift the tariffs they impose upon First World imports while the rich world contrives (through the GATT trade round and the World Trade Organisation which succeeded it) to maintain such barriers on Third World imports into the developed economies.

Paul VI offers no specific 'Catholic answer' to social and economic problems, Filochowski notes. But he does assert that a just
economic order cannot be built on capitalism or on communism.
The Christian cannot adhere to the excessive focus on the individual pursuit of money and power which underlies the ideology of
'liberal capitalism':

> Certain concepts have somehow arisen . . . that present profit as
> the chief spur to economic progress, free competition as the
> guiding norm of economics, and private ownership of the means
> of production as an absolute right, having no limits or concomi-
> tant social obligations. This unbridled liberalism paves the way
> for a particular type of tyranny.[31]

But neither is there a Christian alternative to be found in the denial
of freedom and transcendence and the dialectic of violence in
Marxism:

> It would be dangerous and illusory . . . to accept the elements of
> Marxist analysis . . . while failing to note the kind of totalitarian
> and violent society to which this process leads.[32]

Both unbridled capitalism and totalitarian socialism must go
against a Christian's faith and concept of humanity. And yet Paul
VI knew he must not give up on politics. 'At the main point and
very centre of his Good News, Christ proclaims salvation; this is
the great gift of God which is liberation from everything that
oppresses people,'[33] *Evangelii Nuntiandi* says. Or as *Justice in the
World* puts it: 'action on behalf of justice and participation in the
transformation of the world fully appear to us as a constitutive
dimension of the preaching of the Gospel, or, in other words, of
the Church's mission for the redemption of the human race and its
liberation from every oppressive situation'.[34] An older theology
which saw worldly activity merely as a prelude to the sacred is
here rejected by Paul VI. He goes on to say that at the heart of
the world's structural injustices lies the inability of people to

participate in determining their own destiny. To exercise such practical control over our economic activity *Octagesima Adveniens* calls for the creation of new forms of democracy which involve everybody in a shared responsibility. And yet underlying Paul VI's vision is the same assumption which underlay the Brandt report on North–South relations in 1980 – that the rich could be persuaded to surrender power out of enlightened self-interest. *Octagesima Adveniens*, Filochowski argues, still does not face up to the major issue of confrontation.

Paul VI also developed the doctrine of subsidiarity in an interesting area – that of the internal governance of the church itself. Again it was the Latin American bishops who led the way. At their 1968 conference at Medellín and at its follow-up in Puebla in 1979 they insisted that the church's option for the poor must be expressed not just in words but in the lifestyle of the church itself. They called on the church to revise its own structures, adopt a more austere lifestyle and enable more participation by the poor. It was an agenda to which Paul VI was happy to respond. Each local church has a responsibility to discern the will of God for its local circumstances and to act accordingly; in the face of 'widely varying situations', he concluded in *Octagesima Adveniens*. It is difficult for national churches, therefore, to give 'a unified message . . . which has universal validity'.[35] Hence Christians in Latin America might be entitled to collaborate far more closely with socialist movements than would be appropriate in Europe or North America. *Justice in the World* went further; the church recognized, it said, 'that anyone who ventures to speak to people about justice must first be just in their eyes. Hence we must undertake an examination of the modes of acting and of the possession and lifestyle found within the Church herself'.[36]

It was not a concern which was to be taken up by the next pope. Justice and participation within the church's own structures are not a priority for the more authoritarian John Paul II who, on the contrary, has suppressed 'dissent' and silenced or excommunicated theologians who did not share his hierarchical views. With the election of Cardinal Karol Wojtyla as the first Polish pope in 1978 much changed. The mood of optimism, challenge and confidence which had characterized the developing social teaching was muted. John Paul II, for all his embrace of the Christian virtue of hope, is a man of profound personal and historical pessimism. Progress, he lamented, has become an end in itself to many people. It subordinates 'the whole of human existence to its partial demands, suffocating man, breaking up society, and ending by entangling itself in its own tensions and excesses'.[37] People have become slaves to things. They want to *have* more rather than to *be* more – the hallmark of the consumer society. Moral and technological development are out of kilter. And therefore the international economic order, in which this misdevelopment is rooted, must also be inherently disordered. Evidence of this, the pope says, is the spiralling spending on the arms trade at a time when the needs of the poor are growing – thus making a direct connection between the misuse of the surplus wealth of the rich world and the destitution of millions in the poor world.

A number of elements distinguish the approach of John Paul II, suggests Ian Linden, the director of the Catholic Institute for International Relations (CIIR) in chapter 4 which deals with Pope John Paul's first three major pastoral letters: *Redemptor Hominis* (1979), *Dives in Misericordia* (1980) and *Laborem Exercens* (1981). One is his nationality and the experience of living under totalitarian communism – which means his intellectual discourse is framed in terms of a dialogue with Marxism, though the Polish pope rarely acknowledges this explicitly. It is therefore a dialogue which it is difficult for most in the West to follow. Another is his 'personalist' philosophy which rejects the split between mind and body which has dominated Western thinking since Descartes and instead holds to an 'integral humanism' which declares that human beings are defined by the actions through which they realize their potential. Work for John Paul II is, thus, the quintessential human activity. It is the defining act which makes us fully human. Work expresses human dignity and also increases it. And human dignity and human rights are 'the measure by which social justice can be tested'. This means that people take priority over things and therefore labour must take priority over capital – though John Paul II, Linden argues, ties himself up in knots over this as he tries to avoid sounding like a Marxist. In the end, however, he presents a picture of modern capitalism which suggests that an economic system based on fundamental contradictions – between social justice and efficiency, labour and capital, full employment and the control of inflation – must be inherently flawed. And in this context the pope describes respect for human rights and human dignity as the measure of social justice and elevates the economic and spiritual development of all nations and people to what Linden calls 'the operational principle of human history'.

The indirect employer and structural sin

Among the most significant contributions of John Paul II in these first three encyclicals are their repeated calls to solidarity and their insistence that we must all bear personal responsibility for structural sin. To explain this the pope comes up with the idea of the 'indirect employer'. The direct employer is the owner of some Third World sweatshop who underpays his employees, making it impossible for them to earn a proper wage – a situation which is all-too-common in the poor world. Yet when he is asked why he does this he can reply, with honesty, that he would be priced out of the market if he paid just wages or operated proper health and safety standards. What forces him to do this? Competition from others and the international trading system which promotes it in the face of uncompromising demands from the people who benefit from the unjust situation by buying the cut-price goods. It is that group who are the indirect employer. The pope is clearly talking to Western consumers.

This widening of moral responsibility is an important development in Catholic Social Teaching. It insists that consumers, pension funds, shareholders and multinational firms cannot claim moral neutrality as they go about their business, even if they cannot see those whom their actions might offend. It provides an ethical framework in which to think about commerce and trade, for it extends the idea of moral behaviour far beyond the acts of the mere individual. It facilitates solutions too. It allows for the creation of lobbying groups and 'fair trade' companies who can force changes by persuading consumers with a conscience of the need to shop for a better world, using their economic 'vote' to prefer the good employer over the bad.

One of the most striking features of Catholic Social Teaching, argues the religious commentator and journalist Clifford Longley in chapter 5, is its coherence. Its various principles seem to merge into and arise out of each other, almost as if each concept contains all the others. So if we were to lose one of its principles we could reconstruct it from the others much as we would be able to reconstruct the missing piece of a jigsaw. From the work done by previous popes on the relationship between the pediment of the common good and the two pillars of subsidiarity and solidarity which support it, therefore, John Paul II in the second phase of his social teaching was able to develop more fully the notion of solidarity. He does so by examining its obverse – structural sin. By this he means the accumulation and concentration of many personal sins so that they build up a system which, in its own turn, create 'influences and obstacles which go far beyond the actions and brief life span of an individual'.[38] These, he says in *Sollicitudo Rei Socialis* (1987), amount to 'structures of sin'.

Writing in 1987, two years before the collapse of the Berlin Wall, when the systems of governance of the Cold War remained in place, John Paul II clearly has in mind here the ideologies of communism and capitalism – in both of which he perceives grave deficiencies. Communism is perhaps his chief target, but his criticisms of capitalism are no less scathing:

It is important to note that a world which is divided into blocs, sustained by rigid ideologies, and in which instead of interdependence and solidarity different forms of imperialism hold sway, can only be a world subject to 'structures of sin'. The sum total of the negative factors working against a true awareness of the universal common good, and the need to further it, gives the impression of creating, in persons and institutions, an obstacle which is difficult to overcome.[39]

In both systems the needs of people are subordinated through mechanisms like the arms race or the international financial system to 'the all-consuming desire for profit' or 'the thirst for power, with the intention of imposing one's will upon others'.[40] It leads to idolatry – with money, ideology, class and technology[41] as the new idols.

After the collapse of communism the pope directed his attention to the new unbridled form of capitalism which was claiming its victory over the totalitarian left. In *Centesimus Annus* (1991) Pope John Paul tackles the question of whether the free market might itself be a structure of sin. 'Certainly the mechanisms of the market offer secure advantages, they help to utilize resources better, they promote the exchange of products, above all they give central place to the person's desires and preferences, which, in a contract, meet the desires and preferences of another person.'[42] And he notes there has been some criticism in recent times of the welfare state for sapping ordinary people's initiatives.[43] But, he adds, there are many human needs – like justice and truth – that find no value accorded them in the market.[44] Moreover market mechanisms 'carry the risk of idolatry of the market, an idolatry which ignores the existence of goods which by their nature are not and cannot be mere commodities'.[45] There is, insists Longley, an important distinction to be made between the market as a tool and as an ideology. John Paul II begins to make distinctions between different kinds of capitalism. The obligation to earn one's bread by the sweat of one's brow also presumes the right to do so, concludes the pope:

A society in which this right is systematically denied, in which economic policies do not allow workers to reach satisfactory levels of employment, cannot be justified from an ethical point of view, nor can that society attain social peace.[46]

The use of unemployment as a tool of fiscal management to lower
inflation can never be justified. It can never be, to contradict the
notorious words of the former Chancellor of the Exchequer
Norman Lamont, 'a price worth paying'.

Structural sin requires a structural response. Individuals acting
alone did not create the structures of sin, nor can they – alone –
redeem them. But individuals do try, by trying to help one another.
In *Sollicitudo Rei Socialis* John Paul II insists:

> The fact that men and women in various parts of the world feel
> personally affected by the injustices and violations of human
> rights committed in distant countries, countries which perhaps
> they will never visit, is a further sign of a reality transformed
> into awareness, thus acquiring a moral connotation. It is above
> all a question of interdependence, sensed as a system determin-
> ing relationships in the contemporary world in its economic,
> cultural, political and religious elements, and accepted as a
> moral category. When interdependence becomes recognized in
> this way, the correlative response as a moral and social attitude,
> as a 'virtue', is solidarity.[47]

This solidarity is not a feeling of vague compassion but 'a firm and
persevering determination to commit oneself to the common good;
that is to say, to the good of all and of each individual because we
are all really responsible for all'.[48] This solidarity, which resonates
particularly for a Polish pope because of *Solidarność*, the name
taken by the Polish trade union movement in its struggle for freedom against communism, is the opposite to structural sin. It is also
the means by which men and women must provide that which the
market can never bring to the common good.

Linking sexual and social ethics

Ask most members of the public what they know about the
Catholic Church and they will almost invariably reply that it is
against abortion and artificial contraception. The church's teaching

on sexual and medical ethics is well-publicized, even if many accounts are partial and even distorted. But its social teaching receives little attention from the media and is largely ignored, perhaps because Catholic Social Teaching has always been presented in separate documents and is seen as something apart from other church teaching. That changed with John Paul II's encyclical *Evangelium Vitae* (1995) in which he presents the two as inextricably intertwined. It is the system of democratic capitalism – with its emphasis on economic efficiency, personal freedom and maximum choice – which undergirds a lifestyle in which morality is down-played in all aspects of life. In chapter 6 the moral theologian Julie Clague, of St Mary's University College, argues that *Evangelium Vitae* is, for this reason, perhaps the most important of all John Paul II's encyclicals – because it attempts to draw together politics and economics with medical and sexual ethics into one coherent whole.

The stated focus of the document is 'the value and inviolability of human life'. But in criticizing contemporary Western attitudes to life – which have come to judge its value by utilitarian rather than absolute standards – it extends its scope far wider. The document becomes a critique of the values of the Western lifestyle which has allowed technological and economic progress to push God to the margins. The entire value system of Western society, Pope John Paul II declares, is now dominated by a 'culture of death'. Its values are most evident on questions of the right to life – abortion, euthanasia and other areas where developments in biotechnology create new moral dilemmas. Within this new culture the weak are increasingly under threat from the powerful. For all our contemporary emphasis on human rights, we have also developed a practical disregard for the most fundamental of these human rights – the right to life. This apparent paradox has not come about by accident. Rather it is 'actively fostered by powerful cultural, economic and political currents which encourage an idea of society excessively concerned with efficiency'.[49] Evidence of this is seen, he says, in the way that modern society places work and its fruits – the indulgence of consumer goods and the idea of

personal fulfilment – before the interests of society's most fundamental building block – the family. The consequences for society
are potentially disastrous, for the family plays an essential role in
establishing the opposite of John Paul II's 'culture of death' – the
'culture of life'. Instead of counteracting this many Christians have
taken on the world's priorities and lost sight of their distinctive role
as a counter-cultural corrective.

John Paul's oppositional view of the world, Clague argues, can
tend to distort and simplify positions: church versus world, gospel
versus culture, good versus evil. Such an 'us and them' attitude can
be counter-productive. Most of those who support abortion and
euthanasia, for example, are not totally nihilistic; they believe such
activities promote other values which are important for humanity
and they justify them with arguments about the 'lesser of two
evils'. Arguments with them must begin from a different starting
point than dogmatic assertion. Nonetheless the 'culture of death'
described in *Evangelium Vitae* reflects real tendencies in contemporary society to lose sight of important values or mis-prioritize
them. These stem from the desire to maximize two things – individual freedom and the ability of technology to boost economic
efficiency.

The political problem of mankind is to combine three things –
economic efficiency, social justice and individual liberty – and the
modern age has lost the correct balance between the three elements
of this political equation. On the first of these, *Evangelium Vitae*
says that human needs are being sacrificed to the interests of economic efficiency. Man is being reduced to *homo oeconomicus* with all
progress judged mainly in terms of economic growth. An excessive
emphasis upon efficiency has led to a culture in which others are
considered not for what they 'are', but for what they 'have, do and
produce'. 'The criterion of personal dignity – which demands
respect, generosity and service – is replaced by the criterion of
efficiency, functionality and usefulness,' says *Evangelium Vitae*.
'This is the supremacy of the strong over the weak.'[50]

This process is exacerbated by a mis-emphasis upon the third of
the elements in the political equation – individual liberty. Again

the modern pre-eminence of economics has a role here. The dominant mode of address for individuals in the West has become that of consumer, not citizen, Clague notes. The notion of choice now extends far beyond the supermarket to demands for choice over education, health and other areas of life where issues of communal and social concern also once figured. The deification of efficiency and choice has squeezed out social justice. Indeed in *Evangelium Vitae* John Paul II expresses the fear that an unhealthy desire for absolute freedom and complete control over our lives has become the spirit of the age. Its apotheosis, argues Clague, is the idea of a 'pro-choice' position – whether on abortion or lesser matters – which makes the grounds of any particular choice secondary to the idea of choice itself. Thus choice, she says, has become absolutized.

The job of ethics is to determine which choices are humanizing, and Pope John Paul has doubts that modern democracy has the wherewithal to make that determination. For the pope the weakness of democracy is that public policy is determined by the views of the majority and therefore decisions about the right to life become 'subject to the will of the stronger part'.[51] We are back to the old problem that the common good is not synonymous with the utilitarian notion of 'the greatest happiness for the greatest number'. Democracy, to John Paul's frustration, provides individuals with the freedom to make choices but it has no mechanisms to direct them to chose what is right. The pope is unsure where to go from here. He wants to back democracy for its role in the victory over communism. He wants to say it is preferable to totalitarianism. And yet he wants also to insist that democracies must do certain things – and by insisting paradoxically takes away the freedom intrinsic to the democratic process.

But if *Evangelium Vitae* does not offer a comprehensively satisfactory position on all the issues which John Paul II sets out to address, it does, Clague concludes, clearly carry forward the tradition of Catholic Social Teaching, introducing new themes and fresh emphases. It endorses a vision of the inviolable dignity of the human person and sees them expressed in the secular notion of human rights. It underscores a commitment to the weak and oppressed and calls for the removal of unjust structures which deny basic human rights. It reiterates the basic conviction that the social dimension is essential to human flourishing and that the family is fundamental to that social context.

Globalization and a new morality

There are some indications here of how the church's teaching might help shape the politics of the next century. But John Paul II also turns more directly to the question of the next millennium. In chapter 7 I look at his encyclical *Tertio Millennio Adveniente* (1994). Its focus is not on social teaching – it is preoccupied with preparing the church, rather than the world, for the challenges of the new millennium. But it selects one area for urgent action – Third World Debt which needs to be swiftly alleviated – and in general it calls for a better appreciation and understanding by Christians of the signs of hope present in the last part of the century. Perhaps more significantly it casts further light on Pope John Paul II's difficulty with democracy. Again he complains of religious indifference among Christians, a loss of a sense of the transcendent in human life even among the faithful, and he says ethical relativism, moral uncertainty and theological confusion have entered their thinking. His solution is focussed on Catholics rather than the wider world – calling upon the faithful to return to the sacraments, to promote the family and marriage, and revert to unquestioning fidelity and obedience to the Magisterium of the kind exhibited in former times by the church's martyrs. The chapter also reports on the insights other Christians offer in this tension between the pope's stated preference for democracy and his own wish to make authoritarian impositions upon it. It also looks at how other Catholics are beginning to tussle with a resolution to the tension.

Chapter 7 then looks at the challenges of Catholic Social Teaching in a world economy which is rapidly becoming ever more interdependent and even integrated. It considers the addresses made by John Paul II to the Pontifical Academy of Social Sciences in Rome in 1996 and 1997 in which he tussles with ambiguous feelings about modern capitalism. He continues to express his old reservations about its unchecked excesses, warning of 'the moral principle according to which the demands of the market . . . must not go against the primordial rights of every man to have work through which he can earn a living for himself and his family' but seeming also to endorse the deregulation of the financial markets in the Thatcher and Reagan era which unleashed the forces which brought about globalization: 'the church does not mean to condemn the deregulation of the market itself,' he says, 'but asks that it be envisaged and implemented with respect for the primacy of the human person'.[52] Such globalization is a complex phenomenon but, the chapter goes on to say, its fruits are likely to be most bitter for the world's poor. In the past the relationship between the rich and poor worlds was unfair but clear. The rich world was one of high productivity, high technology and high wages while the poor nations offered low productivity, low technology and low wages. But globalization offers the possibility of high productivity, high technology and *low* wages, threatening the living standards of ordinary people in the industrialized world and the marginalization of those in the poorest countries. The pope is fearful of this. 'The more global the market, the more it must be balanced by a global culture of solidarity, attentive to the needs of the weakest,' he concludes.[53] But his addresses to the Pontifical Academy appear confused about the best way forward.

Much of the thinking about the next steps in the world's political economy is coming from secular philosophers, social scientists and one-time apologists for capitalism. In the book's Epilogue I consider these, along with the implications of globalization for the answers traditionally proposed by social democracy, and the ethical vacuum which is becoming apparent at the heart of post-Enlightenment liberalism. In response to all this, secular thinkers are tentatively venturing out into territory which has already been explored by a century of Catholic Social Teaching, the Epilogue suggests. It then juxtaposes the church's conclusions with contemporary thinking.

It suggests that the tenets of Catholic Social Teaching offer clear pointers in a different direction from contemporary society's continuing emphasis on individual rights at the expense of a sense of social responsibilities. Some of these pointers are self-evident. We need a more inclusive society in which all people are able to take greater control over their lives and to participate more fully in its ordering. Greater democracy, more decentralization, more transparency and greater accountability in government are requisites. So are safety nets for the disadvantaged, but ones which do not rob people of the incentive to work. Society needs a return to an economic and fiscal strategy which puts employment at the top of the political agenda. But there are other requirements which grow from the principles of the church's social teaching. The Epilogue addresses the question of a national minimum wage and, unfashionably, proposes an increase in certain trade union rights. It looks at the need for businesses to become more socially responsible and considers mechanisms of social accounting and ethical consumerism which might create pressure for that. It outlines a number of key changes are needed in the relationship between the First and Third Worlds.

But more than that. Shifts in certain philosophical paradigms are needed, the Epilogue argues. Society needs to reconsider what we mean by economic efficiency. Attention must be given to the way that money has lost its function as the means of exchange and has become instead a commodity; action is needed to dampen the destabilizing affect of large-scale currency speculation. Catholic Social Teaching itself may need to re-examine the breadth of such of its definitions, too, if it is to engage in a fruitful dialogue with secular society. In the journey towards a new politics for the twenty-first century the discourse will inevitably be two way. The Epilogue suggests it has work to do exploring the dynamics of human rights and democracy. There may also be re-thinking to be done on the issue of the family, separating important values from the mere structures which have traditionally carried them.

But most of all Catholic Social Teaching offers pointers to lead us out of the technological determinism and spiritual fatalism which has dogged the latter half of the twentieth century. If it can counter that, and offer a moral compass to the multi-faith pluralist society which will dominate the new millennium, it will make an invaluable contribution to shaping a politics for the twenty-first century. It will inevitably do so in a dialogue with a society of all and no faiths which may necessitate compromises. But what it offers is the tools, if only we have the foresight and the courage to take them up.

Paul Vallely

July 1998

Laying the Foundations:
from *Rerum Novarum* to the Second
Vatican Council

Michael Walsh

The church has always had some form of social teaching. St Paul reflected upon the relationship between Christians and the state in his Letter to the Romans. The fathers of the church were deeply concerned about the morality of ownership of property,[1] of the use of money,[2] and of war and peace.[3] The mediaeval schoolmen had much to say about economics, fixing a just price and agreeing a just wage, and dwelt at length on the propriety of charging interest on loans.[4] And yet the modern church often displays little or no sense of the long history of its own teaching on social issues.

Look up 'colonialism', for instance, in *The New Dictionary of Catholic Social Thought*[5] and you would think that no one had addressed the problem before Pope John XXIII in the 1960s. Yet the Spanish Dominican Francisco de Vitoria, who became the main professor of theology at the University of Salamanca in 1526 and held the post until his death two decades later, had discussed in his *De Indis* and the *De Iure Belli Hispanorum in Barbaros* what right Spain had to invade the New World and to subjugate the inhabitants. He was a staunch defender of the rights of the native peoples, arguing that Spain might rule over them if, and only if, it was for the benefit of the Indians rather than for the profit of the Spaniards. He also suggested that the time might come for an institution such as that of the United Nations – though he wanted to accord it more authority than many would be prepared to defend in this present generation.[6]

De Vitoria is only one example. Not only were there others discussing the same problems in the sixteenth century, but theologians down the ages have examined the moral issues which are faced by the society in which they lived. It should have come as no surprise, therefore, when the Catholic Church in the person of the Bishop of Rome, the pope, began to speak out on social issues. Yet it did. Shock waves were produced by the first of the modern encyclicals on social matters, *Rerum Novarum* (Of New Things) in 1891. The document was all the more startling because it was issued with all the authority – short of the then newly-defined dogma of papal infallibility – of the Vicar of Christ. Though its author, Pope Leo XIII, attacked socialism, his encyclical was itself regarded as socialist.

It was published against the background of two key events: the stirrings of communism across Europe and the unification of Italy. Almost fifty years earlier, in 1848, Karl Marx and Friedrich Engels had published the *Communist Manifesto*, the document which was to undergird the principal programmatic statements of the European socialist and communist parties in the nineteenth and early twentieth centuries. In the years which followed its first printing some church leaders became aware of the challenge socialism was making to take the leadership among the working class. In 1864, the same year that Marx established the First International, Wilhelm von Ketteler, the Bishop of Mainz, produced a book entitled *The Worker Question and Christianity*. His ideas were influenced more by romanticized notions of the structures of mediaeval Germany than by his experience of industrial society, but they were more in sympathy with the ideals of socialism than with the ideology of economic liberalism which then prevailed. In France the *Conseil des Études* followed similar reasoning, and arrived at similar conclusions. There was rather less theory in England but Cardinal Manning won considerable fame both at home and abroad for his arbitration in the London dock strike of 1889. He also made valiant efforts to rally English Catholics to the side of Labour. (His successor as Archbishop of Westminster, Cardinal Vaughan, attributed this to senility.) Across the continent there was wide involvement of the church in social problems.

Private property and public morality

Rerum Novarum, as an encyclical letter, was universal in its scope. But it also reflected local concerns in Italy after the final unification of that country. By 1864 Pope Pius IX had seen the once extensive papal states reduced to Rome and its immediate environs, and it was only with the help of French troops that he held on against the liberal and anti-clerical Piedmontese who were eager for the unification of Italy. Even that modicum was to disappear when the French soldiers were withdrawn because of the Franco–Prussian War and the city of Rome capitulated. On 20 September 1870, after a symbolic resistance by the papal army, the troops of the new national Italian army entered Rome, opening a breach in the wall of Porta Pia. The pope refused to accept the situation, and withdrew inside the Vatican. With the taking of Rome, the unification of the Italian peninsula was completed and the new suffrage produced a parliament which contained significant anti-clerical elements. Among the mainly illiterate masses, preponderantly peasant and Catholic, the first emergings of socialist doctrines began to be discerned.

The creation of the new kingdom of Italy, the country's growing industrialization, and the expansion of the suffrage, all meant that the Italian landowners and nobility no longer had the power to which they were accustomed. Debarred from politics by the *Non Expedit* ('It is not fitting') decree of 1868, many turned to concern for the poor, especially the rural poor. They looked for the restoration of the *ancien regime*, as both a means of improving social conditions for the poor and of restoring their own lost authority. Welfare was for them associated with piety: it had little to do with democracy. Then in 1891, as the Italian Socialist Party was formally constituted, *Rerum Novarum* was published.

Pope Leo XIII was marginally less perturbed than had been his predecessor about the loss of the papal states, but the psychological scars of the event are evident in *Rerum Novarum*. In an earlier encyclical, *Diuturnum Illud*, dated June 1881, just a decade before the publication of *Rerum Novarum*, he had given grudging recognition to the legitimacy of the system of democratic government. But his real sentiments, like his origins, were patrician. He was surrounded by, and took advice from, noblemen and gentry who had been active on behalf of the poor of their respective countries.[7] Leo regarded the church as one of the means to check the advance of communism, and said as much shortly before *Rerum Novarum* was written, in letters to the German Emperor and the Italian government. In January 1901 his encyclical *Graves de communi* contained a warning, directed especially at the French, not to give too radical an interpretation to *Rerum Novarum*.

Obviously, with such a background *Rerum Novarum* was not going to back socialism. Indeed it was in part inspired by the desire to dissuade Catholic workers from allying themselves with socialist movements. The first draft of the encyclical promoted a corporatist regime which harked back to the bygone ideal of an agricultural society ruled by great landowners. That, of course, is what Italy had been before the fall of the papal states. The nation's industrialization, with the exploitation of labour against which the encyclical inveighs, had begun in the North of Italy. Industrial Italy was the new state which had taken over from the popes as the major power in the peninsular. It is that regime which was under attack by Pope Leo. With its condemnation of socialism and its defence of workers' rights, with its regret for the passing of the guilds and its insistence that, in the new workers' associations, spiritual and temporal concerns should be equally prominent, Leo's encyclical was not only criticizing the structures of a new, industrialized Italy, it was also giving support to the traditionalist groups eager to see the restoration of the *ancien regime*. It would be unfair to see what came to be called 'the workers' charter' entirely in that light, but it would be unhistorical to ignore the significance of the Italian context within which the encyclical was composed.

A hundred years on, it is difficult to understand the impact of

Leo's encyclical, so old-fashioned does it appear. It is not just a nostalgia for a mediaeval past. Leo was a great enthusiast for the recovery of the mediaeval theological and philosophical synthesis achieved by the thirteenth-century Dominican, St Thomas Aquinas. Thomism, with its central concept of the 'natural law', was the philosophical tradition in which the encyclical was composed. Natural law, according to Aquinas was 'nothing other than the light of understanding infused in us by God, whereby we understand what must be done and what must be avoided'. It enables us to observe the world and infer from it how God intended it to be ordered. It allowed us to extrapolate the normative from the normal. This tradition, which enabled church thinkers to hold dialogues with secular thinkers in philosophical rather than religious language, has decisively shaped social teaching down to the present day (a tradition which Pope John Paul II has to some extent stepped outside). Also part of the mediaeval vision was the link between guilds and religion: they were to be, at least in part, pious associations: Catholics were to have their own 'associations' (they are not called trade unions) wherever possible. In some countries the establishment at the turn of the century of Catholic trade unionism split the working-class movement. In some places it still survives. One cannot but speculate that the church's loss of credibility with the working class on continental Europe may have had something to do with the divisions which the church, through papal social teaching, forced upon the trade union movement.

Yet, if by 1891 its vision was already anachronistic – with its vocational trade associations which would have united employers and employees in the same union or guild – it opened the way for an endorsement of the development of purely labour unions. And it marked out something which has remained part of papal teaching down to the present day – that the class conflict envisaged in communism has no place in a healthy society. Marxist notions of 'class struggle' were – and are – anathema. The result has been that papal social teaching from Leo XIII onwards has for the most part failed to come to terms with what for most of the century were seen as the competing interests of the different sides of industry. It has been one of the major failures in Catholic social doctrine.

It is closely associated with another great gap: there is in Catholic Social Teaching a great deal about the obligations of wealth distribution but there is little about the obligations of wealth creation.[8] That may be, of course, simply a reflection of the fact that, though there are moral problems aplenty involved in the creation of wealth, most people rarely have to be incited to engage in making themselves rich. By contrast they certainly have to be exhorted to redistribute their wealth to the most needy of society. But the reality was that popes from Leo XIII in 1891 down to Pius XI in 1931 assumed there was no alternative to capitalism and, implicitly, gave it their blessing while, explicitly, exhorting it to behave more responsibly.

That sense of corporatism did not go away. Yet if in conception it was something of a romantic throwback to mediaeval society (or what Thomistic scholars in the nineteenth century thought the Middle Ages to have been like) the ideal and the reality were quite different. It led to the unhappy situation where, as fascism rose to power in Europe in the 1930s, the papacy was seen by many as giving the new dictatorships its backing, and Catholic Social Teaching advocating a Third Way between capitalism and communism which fascism might fulfill.

The principle of subsidiarity

After *Rerum Novarum* the next major statement of Catholic Social Teaching came from Pius XI in *Quadragesimo Anno*, published, as its name indicates (it could be translated as 'Forty years on') to mark in 1931 the fortieth anniversary of *Rerum Novarum*. In the new encyclical corporatism was most ardently advocated and was presented as an alternative to the class struggle:

The State and every good citizen ought to look to and strive towards this end: that the conflict between hostile classes be abolished and harmonious co-operation of the industries and professions be encouraged and promoted . . . In actual fact, human society now, for the reason that it is founded on classes with divergent aims and hence opposed to one another and therefore inclined to enmity and strife, continues to be in a violent condition and is unstable and uncertain . . . As the situation now stands, hiring and offering for hire in the so-called labour market separate men into two divisions, as into battle lines . . . Complete cure will not come until this opposition has been abolished and well-ordered members of the social body – industries and professions – are constituted in which men may have their place, not according to the opposition each has in the labour market but according to the social functions which each performs.[9]

This approach upholds, or seemed to uphold, a stratified, hier-archical society, with every person in his or her own place, being encouraged to sink differences in the interests of peace and harmony. It also requires, though this was certainly no part of Pope Pius's intention as can be seen by the 'principle of subsidiarity' which gets its first mention in the encyclical,[10] a strong state to regulate relations between these groups of industrial or professional interests. And that played right into the hands of Fascism. Fascist organizations which found church support included those associated with Dollfuss in Austria, Salazar in Portugal, Franco in Spain, Petain in Vichy France, Tiso (a Monsignor no less) in Slovakia and, of course, Mussolini in Italy.

Nowhere was church support for Fascism more evident than in Italy. In 1929 the Holy See had negotiated with Mussolini the Lateran Treaty, which established the Vatican City State. Not all Vatican officials were sympathetic to the regime then ruling Italy – Mgr Montini, much later to be Pope Paul VI, was particularly opposed – but others were supportive because, for one thing, the tyranny of Mussolini had not yet been wholly revealed. The form of corporate state which he had created, and which was also at that time to be found in Portugal under Salazar, seemed to be consis-tent with the developing social teaching of the church. At least it avoided the danger of class conflict. Pope Pius XI also recommended a form of economic structure which, he believed, escaped the pitfalls of socialism on the one hand and liberal economics on the other, both of which he roundly condemned.

Quadragesimo Anno was composed two years after the Wall Street crash and the worldwide collapse of money markets in 1929. It was written in the context of economic recession with its inevitable growth of unemployment. Out of the grinding hardship of the working class, as one might have expected, a new sense of strength in solidarity began to develop. Pius XI laid great emphasis, as had Leo XIII, on the continued need for exclusively Catholic trade unions. However much the pope might condemn the abuses of capitalism, and the condemnation is most certainly present in the encyclical, he was not in favour of workers reaching across denominational boundaries to oppose it.

The problem was made all the greater by Pius XI himself. The writing of encyclicals is a confidential business. Authorship is always attributed to the pope, and the identity of those who actually draft them remains usually a closely-guarded secret. In that regard, however, *Quadragesimo Anno* is in a class almost by itself. For in 1971 its author, the Jesuit, Oswald Nell-Breuning, told the story of its compilation in the German Jesuit magazine *Stimmen der Zeit* to mark the encyclical's fortieth anniversary.[11] He revealed that, although the greater part of the text of the encyclical was published as written by himself (the pope corrected the spelling), Pius XI handed to the Jesuit General, who passed on to Fr Nell-Breuning, a small number of paragraphs which he wanted adding. These became paragraphs 91–96, the section of the document most favourable to fascism. After condemning strikes,[12] about which, despite their immense significance in the life of the workers in the later nineteenth century, Leo XIII had been silent in *Rerum Novarum*, Pope Pius XI goes on:

> Anyone who gives even the slightest attention to the matter will easily see what are the obvious advantages in the system we have thus summarily described: The various classes work together

peacefully, socialist organizations and their activities are
repressed, a special magistracy exercises a governing authority.[13]

Why did Pope Pius make these additions which have given him a
largely undeserved reputation for sympathy towards right-wing
dictatorships? The answer may be that he was, within a few weeks
of the publication of *Quadragesimo Anno*, to publish a direct condemnation of fascism in *Non abbiamo bisogno*, an encyclical written,
for obvious reasons, in Italian, and he did not want wholly to
alienate the Italian state under Mussolini's governance. As we have
seen, he had, after all, only a couple of years before in the Lateran
Pacts come to an agreement with Mussolini's government.

That Pius was not sympathetic to the degree of control exercised
by fascist governments is clear in his espousal of the 'principle of
subsidiarity', a principle which has recently received a new lease of
life in the context of the European Union. In essence it states that
a higher authority should not undertake a task that a subordinate
one could perfectly well accomplish. Of it John Coleman, the
editor of *One Hundred Years of Catholic Social Thought*, has
remarked that it is 'neither a theological or even really a philosophical principle, but a piece of congealed historical wisdom.'[14]
The principle of subsidiarity can be found implicitly in *Rerum
Novarum*. There, for example, Leo XIII contrasts the authority of
the father to that of the State.[15] But his point here, and also in the
long discussions[16] about the 'natural right' of workers to unite in
'associations', is to combat socialism, which Leo presents as an all-
pervading authority interfering with every aspect of people's lives.
The vigorous defence of private property[17] is a further example of
this.

Pope Pius describes subsidiarity as 'that most weighty principle,
which cannot be set aside or changed, [which] remains fixed and
unshaken in social philosophy'. And he goes on to define it:

> Just as it is gravely wrong to take from individuals what they can
> accomplish by their own initiative and industry and give it to the
> community, so also it is an injustice and at the same time a grave
> evil and disturbance of right order to assign to a greater and

higher association what lesser and subordinate organizations can do . . . The supreme authority of the State ought, therefore, to let subordinate groups handle matters and concerns of lesser importance . . . those in power should be sure that the more perfectly a graduated order is kept among the various associations, in observance of the principle of 'subsidiarity of function', the stronger social authority and effectiveness will be and the happier and more prosperous the condition of the State.[18]

However enunciated, this is an important practical principle, and one which the church has firmly held on to in its social teaching (even if it has failed, especially in the present pontificate, to apply it to the way the church governs itself). It is a principle which offers a useful yardstick for judging the wisdom of day-to-day decisions in the contemporary political scene. Such a principle would, for example, endorse the local management of schools or the devolution of responsibility to tenants on housing estates.

But the principle can cut both ways. Some activists in the Catholic social movement in England in the 1940s and 1950s, divorcing the notion of subsidiarity from another great principle of Catholic Social Teaching, the common good,[19] argued strongly, in the name of subsidiarity of function, against the creation of the National Health Service and were, in consequence, driven increasingly towards the political right. Moreover subsidiarity can also be employed to justify in broad terms the very unchecked economic liberalism which Pius XI and successive other popes have condemned.

The option of socialism

On socialism Pius XI was even more outspoken than Leo. He wrote in *Quadragesimo Anno*:

If socialism, like all errors, contains some truth (which, moreover, the Supreme Pontiffs have never denied), it is based nevertheless on a theory of human society peculiar to itself and irreconcilable with true Christianity. Religious socialism,

Christian socialism, are contradictory terms: no one can be at the
same time a good Catholic and a true socialist.[20]

In England Cardinal Bourne had immediately to tell Roman
Catholics that these strictures did not apply to the British Labour
Party, and others tried to explain away the condemnations (which
continued throughout the pontificate of the next pope, Pius XII).
So who was this section directed against? There had been socialist
Catholic groups from long before the time of *Rerum Novarum*,
especially in Germany where there was a special consideration.
Fr Nell-Breuning's mentor, the Jesuit Gustav Gundlach, had
written an article warning that the attraction of socialism for
Catholics in Germany might detract from church unity and thereby weaken the (Catholic) Centre Party. It was not surprising, therefore, that Nell-Breuning who, with Gundlach, was close to Centre
Party politicians, used the opportunity of the encyclical to attempt
to strengthen that unity. As John Coleman remarks, 'it is worth
noting how often Catholic statements about socialism have been
tied to the electoral fortunes of confessional parties'; he instances
Pius XII's concern for the Christian Democrats in Italy, the Dutch
bishops in 1952, and the Chilean bishops a decade later.[21] These
interventions, he suggests were 'bent on protecting the standing
Catholic party's electoral chances against defections rather than
really enunciating any issue of high moral principle'.[22] Many
Catholics, unfortunately, are not in a position to distinguish
between the two.

One of the key areas of development by Pius XI was on the
question of private property. The first draft of *Rerum Novarum*
made clear the subordination of private property to the demands of
the common good. But the implication for state ownership and
state intervention brought Catholic teaching too close to socialism
for comfort. The emphasis was therefore changed in the final text
away from the common good to private property. It has taken
almost a century to recover more or less unambiguously, but
without denying the value of private property, the primacy of the
common good over individual rights.[23] It was only with John

XXIII's *Mater et Magistra* that the priority of the common good was fully reasserted.[24]

What resulted from this manipulation of the *Rerum Novarum* passages on private property was a distinctly un-Thomistic approach which made property an almost metaphysical right of the individual, whereas, in the language of scholastic philosophy, it belongs rather to the *bene esse*, than to the *esse* (i.e., to the well being, rather than the essential nature), of the human person. By the time of Pius XI there were theoreticians of Catholic social thought who believed that property which was not used at all, or simply abandoned, might be expropriated. It was against this view that Pius was reacting[25] by insisting that first occupancy, as well as use, constitutes a title to ownership.

When Pope Pius started his commentary on *Rerum Novarum* in *Quadragesimo Anno* he began it with a discussion of workers' associations. Though Leo's 'magna carta of labour fell short of assuring or even recognising the full rights of the worker of its time', as Gordon Zahn has remarked,[26] it did send out shock waves among those who had always assumed that the church would continue to give succour to the rich and the powerful. Now Pope Pius reinforced Leo XIII's support of workers' associations. Admittedly the two pontiffs had different views of the role of workers' unions. For Leo XIII they were ideally formed from both employers and employees. For Pius XI they were the basic constituent of the corporative state. And though neither of these coincided with the role that trade unions came to perform in the post-war world their existence had been papally endorsed and confirmed. They were insisted upon as a natural right, and this at the time was enormously important. So too was Pius XI's grudging concession that Catholics might join secular unions.

There is a significant omission in all this. There was, as John Coleman points out, at least until the 1940s, a lack of any discussion of human rights. Given the emphasis which has been put upon human rights by recent popes, and especially by John Paul II, it is difficult to imagine the church as other than a champion of human rights. But it was not always so, and Pope Pius VI condemned the

French Declaration of the Rights of Man in March 1791.[27] To be fair to Pope Pius, his chief objection was to the Civil Constitution of the Clergy, but in his rejection of that he included a condemnation of, among other things, freedom of religion and of expression. Papal rejection of these human rights, now regarded as fundamental to human dignity, was reiterated in the blanket condemnation of liberalism and the modern age to be found in Pius IX's *Syllabus of Errors* of 1864.

History or blueprint?

No matter how different his approach may be, each pope likes to present his teaching as in direct continuity with that of his predecessors – as is demonstrated by the encyclicals' titles which frequently recall the anniversaries of *Rerum Novarum* to the most recent, *Centesimus Annus*, celebrating its centenary.[28] A pope cannot challenge earlier teaching without calling his own authority into question. Hence the constant reference in these documents to what has gone before. So can the entire corpus of teaching – from that of Leo XIII to the present pope, and encompassing the Industrial Revolution, the rise of communism, the Great Depression, the rise and fall of fascism, the emergence of a post-war economic consensus and its replacement by the neo-liberal Reaganite and Thatcherite global deregulation, and then the fall of communism and the globalization of the world economy – be regarded as constituting a coherent whole which has direct application for our situation today?

Michael Schuck with his volume *That They Be One: The Social Teaching of the Papal Encyclicals, 1740–1989*[29] argued for the coherence of papal social teaching dating from *Ubi Primum* by Benedict XIV. Schuck insists that we need coherence if there is to be rational discussion about the ethical issues involved in the social teaching. This coherence, in the words of John Coleman, commenting on Schuck's book, is 'based in the view of the world as pregnant with the presence of God; in an understanding of the objectivity of moral values and deep concern for protecting the family, religion, and God's purposes for creation; in a sense of unity between the secular and the sacred, their nexus in God's ubiquitous presence'.[30]

So broad a definition of the coherence leaves a great deal of leeway. There is little in such a description which would not be accepted by any Christian – indeed, by any believer in God of whatever faith. It is so general in scope as, to my mind, to be unhelpful in any attempt to provide an overview of papal social teaching. Coleman himself has remarked rather upon the diversity of the teaching: 'A simultaneous reading of the encyclicals . . . shows that various social teachings do not – to obedient or even servile minds and ears – entirely square with one another.'[31]

I am therefore not setting out to oppose either the papacy or papal social teaching when I say that it is important that we should not treat this teaching uncritically, or fail to recognize that it is shaped by particular philosophical, historical and even economic, contexts. We would not do that for the Bible, we would not do it for other papal – or even conciliar – utterances, and we should not do it when faced with the impressive array of documents on society, its rights and its duties, which have been produced by the Holy See over the last hundred years or so. There is something historically specific about the motivations which underlie these early formulations of papal social teaching – with their anachronistic vision of a corporatist Europe and guild-like workers associations, their tendency towards supporting first fascism and then Catholic visions of Christian Democrat political parties, and their shift of emphasis from the common good towards support for the imperatives of private property and capitalist wealth creation. Such teachings, however excellent, are historically conditioned and respond to the needs of the time, as these needs are understood by popes and others who may very well all have their own personal agendas – a fact which is equally true of the popes who succeeded them, as is abundantly evident in Pope John Paul II's *Centesimus Annus* published in 1991 to mark the centenary of *Rerum Novarum*. Those attempting to draw general conclusions must therefore proceed cautiously.

2

Opening the Windows:
John XXIII and the Second
Vatican Council

Brian Davies

It was in the 1960s that a fundamental change occurred which was to mark a turning point in Catholic Social Teaching. Its attitude to the world became more positive and optimistic. It shifted its emphasis away from dependence on the philosophy of natural law – the notion that norms of behaviour could be logically deduced from a study of the essential nature of things – towards listening to human experience and developing a social analysis from that.

It was through Pope John XXIII that the transformation came about. When he was elected many assumed that he was to be a traditionalist caretaker pontiff. But he turned out to be a great reformer who 'opened the windows' to let in the wind of change. Many of the cobwebs of the past were blown away and in came fresh ideas, enabling a new dialogue with the world to take place.

The transition was marked by three major documents: *Mater et Magistra* (1961), *Pacem in Terris* (1963) and *Gaudium et Spes* (1965). The first two were encyclicals of Pope John XXIII written in continuity with the tradition of earlier papal teaching while the third was a pastoral constitution of the Second Vatican Council. Although *Gaudium et Spes* bears the signature of Paul VI and the other 2,300 bishops present, it is a product of Pope John's council and the result of the process of 'aggiornamento' he instigated. As John XXIII's biographer, Peter Hebblethwaite,[1] put it, the

Council acted as the pontificate's 'goal, policy, programme and content'.

It is important not to overstate Pope John's intentions with regard to social teaching. He was certainly not a radical. The process of dialogue with the modern world was begun but it was not at all clear where it would lead. This was a time of transition and reorientation. What was so important at this particular moment was that he was an optimist. It would be for others in later documents to work through the implications of this new stance towards the world. But many of the central themes of more recent social teaching have their roots in this period: the link between the religious and social dimensions of life, the dignity of the human person, the recognition of political and economic rights, the promotion of the common good, the option for the poor, the importance of political participation and the promotion of peace.

In 1961, for the seventieth anniversary of *Rerum Novarum*, John XXIII wrote an encyclical reviewing the major points of the earlier teaching of Leo XIII (1871–1903) and Pius XI (1922–1939). This was *Mater et Magistra* (Mother and Teacher), and though there is some updating there is not really a great deal in subject matter that is new. What makes the difference is the tone. It relates to the world at the start of the 1960s in a positive, affirming way, welcoming what is good wherever it is to be found in the midst of the changes of technical, social and political life.

If John XXIII repeats earlier teaching on the value of private property, private initiative and just remuneration for work, through it all he indicates a break in the alliance that had existed with socially conservative forces. Employees, for example, should have some share in their companies (management, profits and even ownership) – the benefits should not accumulate just for the owners of capital. Indeed, workers should have some say in policy at national level. The state should also play a more active role in controlling major companies and, for the common good, may even take over the means of production as long as the principle of subsidiarity is observed. However challenging these proposals might have been in the 1960s, they are even more striking in the political context of the world in the 1990s where, across the globe, workers have been progressively disempowered and privatization of national industries is the order of the day.

While restating the permanent validity of the right to private ownership, the pope insists that this right applies to everyone. This means there is a fundamental obligation of granting to all an opportunity to own property. In other words there is need of wider distribution 'to all classes of people'. He insists also on the obligations of ownership: all of this world's goods are intended for the support of the whole human race. In owning them we are 'stewards of God's providence for the benefit of others'. Private ownership no longer sounds quite so private.

Solidarity and social relationships

Much discussion has centred on one particular passage of *Mater et Magistra* which runs as follows:

> Certainly one of the principal characteristics which seem to be typical of our age is an increase in social relationships, in those mutual ties, that is, which daily grow more numerous and which have led to the introduction of many and varied forms of associations in the lives and activities of citizens, and to their acceptance within our legal framework . . . This development in social life is at once a symptom and a cause of the growing intervention of the State, even in matters which are of intimate concern to the individual, hence of great importance and not devoid of risk.[2]

Early translations used 'socialization' where the text speaks of 'an increase of social relationships'. This led some commentators in the media to suggest that, since Pope John goes on to approve of this development, the encyclical was in effect proposing some form of socialism. 'Socialization' had its origin rather in the thinking of the early twentieth-century French philosopher Pierre Teilhard de Chardin for whom the interlocking of human destinies through technological developments was a form of spiritual progress. There were dangers, of course, of excessive interference with personal responsibilities and of increased bureaucracy, but the pope evidently considered the promotion of personal welfare and of community living to be more important. The passage quoted above goes on to cite examples of state intervention such as 'health and education, the choice of a career, and the care and rehabilitation of the physically and mentally handicapped'. As an expression of the common good, and with appropriate checks and balances, John XXIII is clearly approving of the welfare state – something about which John Paul II expresses much stronger reservations in a more recent social encyclical.[3] But against any accusation of socialism John XXIII also urges governments to strike a balance in all this between the collaboration of individuals and co-ordination by the state.

Mater et Magistra does raise some new issues, though for the main part they are explored much more fully in later documents. The pope reflects for example on the mass migration taking place from the land – a phenomenon which has greatly intensified and as the century draws to a close is now an acute problem in many parts of the Third World – and sees agriculture as a depressed sector needing support and modernization. His emphasis in the way this is treated is on orderly and balanced development in parallel with what is happening in the rest of the economy. If agriculture is lagging behind industry and services (the other areas of production), then it should be brought into line. The principles to be applied are the traditional ones: with the common good in mind, public authority should support private enterprise to achieve economic and social balance in the community while observing subsidiarity.

The problem is viewed internationally: some countries are using primitive agriculture to produce insufficient food for the population, whereas other countries using modern methods produce great surpluses. The solidarity of the human race demands that this discrepancy be eliminated. All that is needed is that people all over the world actively co-operate. Indeed, the answer is obvious – if only power politics and vested interest did not enter into it. The difficulty which the pope does not adequately address is that both politics and vested interests do nowadays enter in – and the intervening years have only underscored the fact – with the enormous and increasing power exercised by transnational agribusinesses and the continuing role of vast agricultural subsidies by the United States and Europe which discriminate massively against the small family-run farms of the Third World.

It is in this encyclical that a pope for the first time deals with the issue of aid. Catholic Social Teaching thus begins to assume a wider international scope than before. Again the general approach is to draw attention to the obvious ideal solution. What is needed, the pope says, is an education of conscience regarding the responsibility of those with more of the world's goods. Aid should be made available for a country's own growth under its own control, without attempting to exercise political influence. Indeed, anything that undermines national integrity is immoral. The least developed countries often preserve an ancient tradition and essential human values: aid must not be used to dominate or undermine them. Looking back at this section in the light of the models of development which Western nations impressed upon the Third World, in particular the neo-liberal free market solutions imposed in the 1980s and 1990s, John XXIII's treatment of aid seems not only optimistic but rather naive.

But perhaps the issue that is dealt with least satisfactorily is population. Arguments concerning the disproportion between population and food supply Pope John sees as depending on unreliable data. The resources of nature we are told are well-nigh inexhaustible and they can always be exploited to human advantage: a provident God grants sufficient means to find a solution. In any case no solution is acceptable which does violence to human dignity. There was perhaps a hint here of the thinking which was six years later to lead Paul VI in *Humanae Vitae* to overturn the recommendations of a papal commission which had proposed that the church should henceforth permit artificial contraception. It was to prompt widespread dissent throughout the church.

Much of the final chapter of *Mater et Magistra* is devoted to the nature and importance of Catholic Social Teaching itself. It is just not possible, the pope asserts, to deal adequately with the temporal order without God. Attempts to do so by contemporary ideologies end up by failing to take the whole person into account. The human person is therefore the foundation, cause and purpose of all social institutions. This principle is the basis of Catholic Social Teaching which is integral to the Christian understanding of human life. It should be taught at all levels in the church and so be put into practice. The process is for everyone to examine their social condition, evaluate the principles involved and so decide how to act – a principle articulated in the 'see, judge, act' methodology developed by the founder of the Belgian Young Catholic Workers' movement, Mgr Joseph Cardijn, for use with groups of workers and students. It is the method widely employed in basic Christian communities throughout much of the Third World and is what lies behind 'the pastoral cycle' used by the Justice and Peace groups established by the church since Vatican II.[2]

Everything follows from the right ordering of society, John XXIII concludes. In this the pope identified with the traditional natural law approach of his predecessors. But the style of *Mater et Magistra* was different. The church was beset by so many new problems that, according to some, people were in danger of losing their human identity. Yet the modern world was greeted with a spirit of optimism. What comes through, just as in his personal dealings, is the sheer goodness of Pope John. Overall, this change of tone was a great success and the encyclical was well received.

Human dignity and human rights

John XXIII's second contribution to social teaching came only two years later. *Pacem in Terris* (Peace on Earth) was written during the first year of the Vatican Council and was published just a few months before the pontiff's death by which time he had become highly popular, making an enormous impact by the sheer force of his personality. This was a time of mounting world tension. He was

much involved in diplomacy over the Cuban Missile Crisis in 1962
and a little earlier the Berlin Wall had been erected. It is a measure
of the increasing role the papacy was playing in world events that
in nineteen years his predecessor Pius XII – no mean diplomat –
met with some eight heads of state; in five years Pope John met
with thirty-eight. All the indications are that he worked hard at
counselling peace and restraint and that he was taken seriously.
This was also a time of wide-ranging activity within the church. As
well as convening the council, he had appointed many Third
World bishops, fostered closer co-operation with the Orthodox
and set up a new Secretariat for Christian Unity, with official
representation at the World Council of Churches.

Although there had been an attempt near the beginning of the
council to ensure that the church did not deal only with internal
matters but should also address issues '*ad extra*' – those which
concerned the wider world – it was not to be till the very end
of the council's deliberations that space could be found to discuss
its document on 'The Church in the Modern World' which
eventually became *Gaudium et Spes*. Although he could not know
how imminent his death would be, the pope perhaps did know that
his own days were limited. He felt that a fresh plea for peace could
not wait. To a world much threatened by war (even nuclear war)
he had something important to say and, for the first time in an
encyclical, he addressed not only Christians but 'all people of good
will'.

Peace requires the observance of divinely-established order.
This is according to natural law and, as such, is inscribed in the
heart of everyone. In this way, the encyclical presents a philosophy
of rights and duties to be observed by individuals, public authorities, national governments and the world community. The argument flows from the human person, having intelligence and
free-will, who therefore has universal and inalienable rights and
duties. What helps the person to grow is good; what inhibits and
destroys is bad.

Pacem in Terris therefore presents a list of rights and corresponding duties:

- The right to life and the means to sustain it, including basic security.
- The right to one's good name, to investigate the truth in freedom, to have access to information, and to share in the benefits of culture.
- The right to worship God according to one's conscience.
- The right to choose one's state in life, including the right to establish a family or pursue a religious vocation.
- Economic rights, including the right to work, the right to a just wage, and the right to hold private property – with its social obligations.
- The right to meet with others and form associations.
- The right to freedom of movement, including the right to emigrate and immigrate
- Political rights, including the right to take an active part in public life and the right to the legal protection of one's rights.[5]

The pope emphasized that these are inalienable rights that flow from the very nature of the human person. Of particular interest, therefore, in the light of widespread unemployment throughout the world over the past two decades, is that work is seen to be a right. Even more challenging, perhaps, with ever-increasing numbers of refugees and asylum-seekers moving to the Western world and across the Third World, is that freedom of movement is, again, seen to be an inalienable right, one which most Western governments seem reluctant to incorporate into their immigration policies.

The church did not practice everything the pope preached. Some of the theologians censured by Rome during the pontificate of the authoritarian Pope John Paul II must have reflected with disbelief on the teaching that 'to investigate the truth in freedom' was a matter of right. There are also rights which are remarkable for their omission, like the rights of the child and the right of women to equal treatment; the need to express rights in this way has perhaps become clearer as we have become more sensitized to their abuse. But whatever reservations might be expressed about the items included in the list, the key point was the fundamental place that human rights have in the overall argument of the encyclical.

The document makes three observations about the contemporary world. Firstly, the material condition of working people has greatly improved. Secondly, women are demanding and playing a more active role in public life. Lastly, all nations are becoming more independent. All of these are seen as signs of liberation and all are positively affirmed. The contrast with the older style is apparent. In the past, reflection on 'the signs of the times' would almost certainly have been a prelude to various denunciations.

What the pope is saying is that good things are happening in the world which are not a result of the church's activity. On the contrary, he says, the world is teaching the church, which therefore needs to be open to the action of the Spirit in history. 'Human society is primarily a spiritual reality in which truth is shared, rights and duties expressed . . . and a means of passing on to others all that is best in the world.'[6]

With such an ideal about the nature of society, it is clear then why the infamous suggestion by Margaret Thatcher that 'there is no such thing as society'[7] is completely unacceptable. It is not just that society and the common good are part of the language of social teaching, but society is 'a spiritual reality' through which we may discern the activity of God's Spirit. This whole theme is fully adopted in the council's document on 'The Church in the Modern World', which eventually became *Gaudium et Spes*.

Authority is necessary for the proper functioning of society and its binding force is derived from the moral order which has God as its source. The appeal to work for the common good is made to people's conscience, which is informed by right reason. Here lies the sole purpose of civil authority: the attainment of the common good of human beings. It cannot function by means of threats and rewards for these provide no incentive to work for the common good.

The state and the option for the poor

The document goes on to present what amounts to the requirement for public authority to make an option for the poor.

> Every civil authority must strive to promote the common good in the interests of all, without favouring any individual citizen or group of citizens . . . Nevertheless, considerations of justice and equity can at times demand that those in power pay attention to the needs of the weaker members of society, since these are at a disadvantage when it comes to defending their own rights and asserting their legitimate interests.[8]

We have here a clear expression of the rationale for the whole idea of the option for the poor which was to occupy such a central place in later social teaching.

The relation between authority and citizens can be seen in terms of rights and duties. For good government there should be a charter of rights and a written constitution recognizing the nature and limits of its sphere of activity – something which the United States has enshrined in law and a framework for which is set out in various European institutions though which the British Government has displayed a historic reluctance to incorporate. The task of civil authority then is to maintain balance so that the rights of one group are not at the expense of another.

The line of argument is straightforward: what has been said at the level of individuals can be applied to the relations of political communities with each other. The common good of the state must be seen in the wider context of the common good of humanity. This principle leads immediately to two conclusions. Firstly, every trace of racial discrimination must be eliminated for all states and individuals are equal in dignity. Secondly, every state has the right to exist and to develop along lines that it determines for itself, as long as this does not conflict with the good of others. There is therefore a corresponding obligation for states that are more developed 'to make a greater contribution to the common cause of social progress'.[9]

Pope John draws particular attention to the plight of increasing numbers of refugees, many of whom had been exposed to great suffering. Refugees cannot lose their rights simply because they are deprived of citizenship of their own states. These rights include 'the right to enter a country in which they hope to be able to provide more fittingly for themselves and their dependants'.[10] There is therefore a duty on the part of the state to accept such immigrants and, always bearing in mind the common good of the whole community, enable them to develop as members of the society they have chosen. In a world where the number of refugees has increased enormously in recent years, but so too have the restrictions on entry, the emphasis placed here on a refugee's fundamental right is striking. Such a position goes against the received wisdom of the times after nearly four decades. As the end of the century approaches politicians continue to discriminate between what they call 'genuine asylum seekers' and 'economic migrants'. Catholic Social Teaching clearly challenges the distinction. To advocate a shift in national policies to accommodate this papal insight might not be deemed politically realistic in the short-term but it does points us towards a very different norm from the one now commonly accepted.

Another particular issue taken up by the encyclical is that of the arms race which involves a vast outlay of resources which could be used to help less developed countries.

> Even though the monstrous power of modern weapons does indeed act as a deterrent, there is reason to fear that the very testing of nuclear devices for war purposes can, if continued, lead to serious danger for various forms of life on earth. Hence justice, right reason, and the recognition of human dignity cry out insistently for a cessation to the arms race.[11]

The same message, repeated many times in the years that have followed, has been largely ignored. 'True and lasting peace among nations cannot consist in the possession of an equal supply of armaments but only in mutual trust.'[12]

There is some evidence of limited progress in this area. The

International Monetary Fund and World Bank have begun to require that Third World governments in search of loans scrutinize their defence spending even as they were required in the 1980s and 1990s to make cuts in their education and health budgets to enable them to pay the installments due on earlier loans. Donor countries now speak of attaching 'good governance' conditions to future aid which may be structured to encompass more prudence in spending on arms though inevitably such requirements may yet need to go much further.

With growing interdependence, John XXIII argues, no state can pursue its own interests in isolation from the rest. On the other hand, national governments are inadequate to the task of promoting the universal common good. What is needed is a world-wide public authority set up by general consent. John XXIII therefore gives strong support to the United Nations as the only body which in principle could maintain peace between nations. In order to do this the UN would need progressively to adapt its structures and methods of operation so as to be able effectively to safeguard the personal rights of every human being. In the intervening years there have been developments here too, though ones which Pope John would not have welcomed. For while governments have continued to look to the UN to exercise such a role, in practice the power and the resources have been denied the UN by those same governments, led by the United States, which has withheld its subscriptions to a larger degree than any other nation.

Ultimately *Pacem in Terris* is an argument and a plea for peace based on human rights. By using a natural law approach, based therefore on reason rather than revelation, it is able to address itself to all people of good will. At the same time, however, this is a deeply Christian text which recognizes that peace is a gift of God which has to be prayed for. Genuine and lasting peace has to come from within, from a change in people's hearts. Such peace depends on an order that is 'founded on truth, built upon justice, nurtured and animated by charity, and brought into effect under the auspices of freedom'.[13] This, in short, is the peace that Christ came to bring but 'is not as the world gives it'.[14]

The changing church in a changing world

Pacem in Terris received widespread acclaim – and not just among
Catholics. Its optimistic tone, taking the modern world seriously
and appraising it positively, had a powerful effect on public
opinion. In the midst of mounting tension and the threat of war it
presented a long-term vision of a world people hardly dared think
possible. But the most important in status of all the documents of
Catholic Social Teaching is *Gaudium et Spes* (1965). Promulgated
the day before the Vatican Council ended this 'pastoral constitution', as the product of debate and reflection of a pope in council,
represents the opinion of the overwhelming majority of the world's
bishops. It had for its scope all the church's dealings with the
modern world. However it must be confessed that apart from its
opening sentence – of which more shortly – it is not widely
quoted. In trying to deal with everything it ended up as a very
lengthy, repetitive text that the council fathers did not have time to
edit properly and make concise.

At the outset of the council there was no such item on the
agenda at all, but at the end of the fateful opening session which
fundamentally changed the whole process and content of debate,
Cardinal Suenens proposed that the council should consider not
just internal matters but the church's relations *ad extra*. Helped by
the council's opening 'Message to Humanity' which highlighted
peace and social justice as urgent issues to be addressed, the Co-
ordinating Commission adopted the proposal. It was referred to
initially as Schema XIII, then as 'The Church in the Modern
World'. The draft did not get discussed till the final session, by
which time not only had *Pacem in Terris* been published but a new
pope, Paul VI, had delivered a highly successful address to the
United Nations on Peace.

When it was published as *Gaudium et Spes* it repeated the themes
of John XXIII's two social encyclicals, endorsing the optimism and
positive attitude towards the world that he had encouraged. At the
same time the document tempered that optimism by contrasting
the harsh world of reality with the ideals for which to strive. It

proposed a liberal agenda rather than a radical one but this provided a basis for the more radical teaching which was to come through the writings of Paul VI.

The opening words of the document indicate from the outset the extent to which the church identifies with the human condition. They also include a statement of what was to become a growing emphasis on the option for the poor:

> The joys and the hopes, the griefs and the anxieties of the people of this age, especially those who are poor or in any way afflicted, these are the joys and hopes, the griefs and anxieties of the followers of Christ.[15]

The root reason for human dignity is the call to communicate with God. The stress is on the fact that, however much conflict there might have been in human history, human beings are nonetheless created in God's image and are therefore free to act according to conscience, which is described as a person's 'most secret core and sanctuary'. It is the same line of argument as was used in the Council's Declaration on Religious Freedom.

Faced with modern forms of atheism, the council did not issue anathemas and condemnations as earlier councils might have done. Rather its document recognizes how weighty are the questions which atheism raises and insists that the church is ready to enter into dialogue. In fact, earlier in the same year as the promulgation of the Constitution, the Vatican set up a Secretariat for Non-believers.

The theme of socialization, already raised by John XXIII, was taken up by the council. Technological changes have created interdependence, but to a large extent without fostering interpersonal relationships. If we recognize that the progress of the human person and the advance of society hinge on one another, we can achieve a truly human world community with individuals playing their part responsibly. The approach here is optimistic, but there is concern that individuals could become merely 'cogs in the machine'.

The more humble tone adopted by Pope John is also continued. Respect and love are due to those who think differently – even to those who are perceived to be in error. This fundamental distinction between the person and what he or she holds may seem obvious but it was an enormous step forward, making genuine dialogue possible. There is a clear recognition that the church does not have all the answers but, by drawing moral and religious principles from the Word of God, she does have something to contribute to temporal affairs and to making the human family more human. At the same time the church is humbly aware of what she may learn: her intention in all this is that God's kingdom may come and the whole human race be saved.

Of the subjects raised for pastoral reflection the most urgent is seen to be that of the family which is the foundation of society. The document considers the factors that are causing the breakdown of marriage and family life and presents the Christian understanding of marriage. The emphasis here is on the centrality of conjugal love and the covenant relationship between the spouses, going far beyond the artificiality and legalism of earlier pronouncements about the primary and secondary ends of marriage. Of its nature, the document says, marriage must be open to children, but responsible parenthood is advocated. How exactly this is to be achieved is not discussed, for this matter had been put in the hands of the Special Commission set up by John XXIII in 1963. It was not to produce its report till after the council had ended. It was Pope Paul VI's reaction to that which was to produce the controversial condemnations of artificial contraception in *Humanae Vitae*.

Gaudium et Spes recognizes a new age in human history characterized by profound changes in the way people strive to control the world. Urbanization and industrialization in particular have had an enormous impact on people's lives. As a contemporary human culture emerges, it is essential that the Christian maintains contact with all aspects so that it can foster the development of the whole.

This was the first foray by social teaching into such an all-embracing area of reflection and it is sometimes regarded as not having been very successful. Most of the points made are too general and often too obvious to have much impact. One specific conclusion drawn, however, is that, in order to be abreast of developments in culture, people should be free to search for truth and express their opinions. The council insists that this applies also within the church. 'Let it be recognized that all the faithful, whether clerics or laity, possess a lawful freedom of inquiry, freedom of thought and of expressing their mind with humility and fortitude in those matters on which they enjoy competence.'[16] Theologians who have been called to account in more recent years by Cardinal Ratzinger's Congregation for the Doctrine of the Faith must have wondered what these words really meant.

While recognizing a fundamental imbalance between wealth and poverty in the world, the document is optimistic about the reform of the world's economic structures, but it is less clear about how this is to be done. There is an assumption that the best way for the Third World to attain social justice is through Western-style development. The subordination of individual rights to the collective organization of production is rejected. On the other hand, worker participation and profit-sharing are commended.

The right to private property is once again upheld, but only after stress is laid on the common destiny of all earthly goods. It quotes from the twelfth-century founder of the study of canon law, the Italian monk Gratian: 'Feed the man dying of hunger because if you have not fed him, you have killed him.'[17] The obligation to help the poor goes beyond doing so merely out of one's superfluous goods. The strongest statement is made with regard to those in extreme necessity: in such circumstances they have the right simply to take what they need. What exactly would be legitimate in this connection is not made clear.

The council is open to the idea of communitarian ownership (as was traditional in Africa and was being tried in new forms there); and it makes a rather careful statement on the need for land reform without indicating how it would be brought about. In the case of oppression of citizens by a public authority, 'it is legitimate for them to defend their own rights and the rights of their fellow citizens against the abuse of this authority'.[18] But again it is not clear what would be justifiable, only that it would need to be 'within those limits drawn by the natural law and the gospels'.

On the subject of peace, *Gaudium et Spes* repeats much of what had already been said in Pope John's *Pacem in Terris* but with a fuller theological basis. Peace is not merely an absence of war but has to be built on an order brought about by people's thirst for justice. Although peace at one level is a gift of God, it still has to worked for, defended and constantly renewed. Governments cannot be denied the right to legitimate self-defence as long as there is a lack of a sufficiently powerful authority at the international level to safeguard security. The arms race as a way of preserving peace is rejected, and the council praises those who renounce violence in defence of their rights. Meanwhile everyone should work for disarmament and the change of attitude needed. A more peaceful world can only be brought about by addressing economic inequalities and the underlying injustices. The council gave rise to the formation of Justice and Peace organizations at various levels in the church; since then the fact that there is a necessary connection between Justice and Peace has been a fundamental insight of Catholic teaching.

The document hinted at the need for further reform. It pronounced that the church stood ready to renounce even her legitimate rights where they may 'cast doubts on the sincerity of her witness'.[19] It was a recognition that the church had to subject itself to the same critique which it applied to others. The church's own lifestyle and power structures had to alter where they were in conflict with the message of justice and peace. It did not, yet, go beyond words. But at the end of this period John XXIII and the Second Vatican Council had fundamentally redefined something at the heart of Catholic Social Teaching. More than that they had redefined what was understood by 'church'. The church was no longer thought of as 'a perfect society', as turned in on its sacramental life, as centralized and defensive. Rather it was perceived as open to the world, where God's Spirit could be discerned in the midst of the joys and the sufferings of the age. The contribution of this era to the development of Catholic Social Teaching also involved a changed methodology which was intimately linked with these changes in understanding. The methodology involved a gradual move away from a deductive 'natural law' approach to a more experiential process of 'reading the signs of the times' along with pastoral planning and action.

What this period's three key documents have to say on any specific issue may largely have been superseded. Even so they marked a profound shift in the relationship between the church and the world – and the way each regarded the other. The world was no longer seen mainly in terms of threat and evil, confined with politics to the private arena, but as part of God's continuing creation for whose transformation we take responsibility, perceived therefore as a source of optimism. And the church was seen by the world as interacting with the realities of secular life.

There may be those who will argue that in more recent years, under the authoritarian pessimism of Pope John Paul II, the pendulum has been swinging in the opposite direction. But the changes under John XXIII and Vatican II constituted a turning point. That fundamental shift – with its continuing insistence that the church must direct itself towards 'the option for the poor' through whom God is revealing himself – offers lasting pointers towards how the relationship between the church and the world must continue to develop in the next century.

3

Looking out to the World's Poor: The Teachings of Paul VI

Julian Filochowski

It has been the fate of Pope Paul VI to be caricatured, scorned and dismissed by many within and beyond the church as 'the pope who said "No" to artificial birth control'. Yet Paul VI was one of the great popes and history will judge his as a great pontificate. John XXIII had opened the window which for centuries had stood closed between the church and the world. Paul VI looked out and saw the world's poor. But he also saw that the church could no longer have universally valid solutions to every social problem. His pontificate (1963–1978) clarified the role of the church in meeting its responsibilities in a world of rapid change.

After the glut of conciliar texts produced by the Second Vatican Council, Paul VI could have sat on his laurels with the perfectly understandable excuse of avoiding doctrinal indigestion in the body of the church. But he did not. In a turbulent period of political upheaval and headlong social change Catholic Social Teaching developed dramatically and visibly. Even excluding the Vatican Council's Pastoral Constitution on the Church in the Modern World, *Gaudium et Spes* (December 1965), Paul VI's was a pontificate with an unparalleled output of documents on Catholic Social Teaching: *Populorum Progressio* – on development among the world's poor nations (March 1967), *Octagesima Adveniens* – a call to action (May 1971), *Justice in the World* from the Synod of Bishops (November 1971) and *Evangelii Nuntiandi* on evangelization (December 1975).

The two pillars of Catholic Social Teaching are solidarity – the notion that we are all responsible in some way for one another – and subsidiarity – the idea that political and social decisions should be taken at the lowest level possible, consonant with good government. These two principles are always in some sense in tension, perhaps in dialectical tension. The East–West conflict and the threat of totalitarian communist regimes had brought to Catholic Social Teaching a particular emphasis on the subsidiarity side of the equation. Under Paul VI there was now a redressing of the balance towards solidarity, with a shift in focus to our duties in relation to the community, to society and to the global family.

Only fifteen months after the publication of *Gaudium et Spes*, Pope Paul VI produced a social encyclical. The impulse to focus on development had come from his visit to India in December 1964. From his meetings with the Latin American bishops during the council he had realized that, though *Gaudium et Spes* was full of optimism about the church's impact on the world, it was weak on economic analysis. Paul VI therefore addressed in *Populorum Progressio* what was clearly the social problem of the age – the division between the rich and the poor nations. Its tone is alternatively plaintive, angry, and urgent.

Previous encyclicals had inevitably been written from a predominantly European perspective; *Populorum Progressio* attempts to be truly catholic and planetary. In looking at relations between rich and poor, powerful and powerless, *Populorum Progressio* does at the global level what *Rerum Novarum* did at the national. It reflects the thinking of the Dominican Louis Lebret, who had been summoned by Pope Paul to be a *peritus* (theological consultant) at the Council and who had been a great help on his mission to the UN in New York to appeal for peace. *Populorum Progressio* made a great impact. I remember well as a university student reading extracts from it in *The Guardian* – and felt proud to be a Catholic. François Perroux, Professor at the College de France, regarded it as 'one of the greatest texts of human history' – a profound and original synthesis of the Ten Commandments, the Gospel teaching and the Declaration of Human Rights. On the other hand the *Wall Street Journal* regarded *Populorum Progressio* as 'warmed-over

Marxism' since it rejected the 'trickle down' theory of development which leaves everything to market forces and assumes that
some part of the benefits reaped by the rich will eventually trickle
down to the poor. Paul VI particularly incensed the free marketeers
when he asserted:

> We must repeat once more that the superfluous wealth of rich
> countries should be placed at the disposal of the poor nations
> . . . Besides, the rich world will be the first to benefit as a result.
> Otherwise their continued greed will certainly call down on
> them the judgement of God and the wrath of the poor, with con-
> sequences no one can foretell.[1]

Populorum Progressio criticizes capitalism more strongly than
earlier Catholic Social Teaching – including in its critique the
profit motive and the unrestricted use of private property. Paul
VI's support for land reform was audacious and hit a raw nerve in
Latin America, where so much land is concentrated in very few
hands and where expropriation was (and in some places still is)
regarded as pure and unadulterated Leninism. Equally significant
were his discussions of the restriction of capital flows and of industrialization.

In a notable advance on earlier documents Paul VI does not provide solutions before first seeking to analyse the causes for the
imbalance between rich and poor. In examining the causes of
poverty and justice he highlights: the legacy of colonialism, which
is nuanced as he underlines that it brought benefits as well; the
present neo–colonial situation which has largely replaced it; and the
imbalance of power between nations.

Populorum Progressio challenges the view that the former
colonies have in the long run benefited by being brought into the
mainstream of modern civilization. Particularly debilitating has
been the total dependency of many countries on a single export
crop.[2] As indications of neocolonialism, *Populorum Progressio* refers
to regimes where a small privileged élite holds a monopoly of
wealth and power.[3] At the international level, trading relations are

such that 'poor nations become poorer while the rich ones become still richer'.[4] Clearly it is not to be assumed that poverty and under-development result from natural causes or laziness.

The structures of injustice

What is called for evidently is a change in the structures. 'The rule of free trade, taken by itself, is no longer able to govern international relations' and therefore 'the fundamental principle of liberalism (as it is called) as the norm for market dealings is open to serious question'.[5] International trade is unjust because there is a growing inequality between the trading partners. So free trade can be called just only when it conforms to the demands of social justice.[6] Free trade remains subordinate to the principle that the earth and all it produces are intended for the benefit of all. The same kind of support system which operates within wealthy countries towards the weaker sections of the economy should be introduced on a global scale between rich and poor countries.[7]

This is the most trenchant part of Paul VI's encyclical. The proposals are very close to those demands made some years later by developing countries as part of a 'New International Economic Order'. What *Populorum Progressio* has to say about free trade is highly relevant in the 1990s when the market has been transformed into an idol and we have trade which is neither free nor fair.

Not that Paul VI has a specific 'Catholic answer' to social and economic problems. What he condemns are the injustices perpetrated by unjust capitalistic trading[8] and he asserts that a just economic order cannot be built on liberal capitalism.[9] He proposes instead the guiding principles of solidarity between rich and poor[10] and of dialogue[11] leading to planning on a global scale.[12] For this to happen there is a need for some sort of world authority.[13] Paul VI had already argued for this in his UN address. Within this analysis Paul VI addresses a host of issues which recur today: the indivisibility of economic development and social progress; the temptation by the Third World to copy or mimic the rich countries; the obligation of the rich to offer aid; the overriding dignity of the worker; family planning; creativity in society and the role of missionaries in development.

Paul VI acknowledges that he cannot enforce a new international order. He can only appeal – to Catholics, to Christians and to all people of good will[14] – and offer arguments based on justice and self-interest. What is at stake is not just the life of the poor and civil peace in the developing countries but, ultimately, world peace: 'Development is the new name for peace'.[15] Those who fail to respond call down God's judgment, Paul VI warns, and the wrath of the poor.[16] He offers no further teaching on a violent reaction from the oppressed. He simply warns of the risk:

> Lacking the bare necessities of life, whole nations are under the thumb of others; they cannot act on their own initiative; they cannot exercise personal responsibility; they cannot work towards a higher degree of cultural refinement or a greater participation in social and public life. They are sorely tempted to redress these insults to their human nature by violent means.[17]

At once the Pope goes on to point out that a revolutionary uprising only produces greater misery. But in this rejection of revolution he does make an exception: '. . . where there is manifest, long-standing tyranny which would do great damage to fundamental personal rights and dangerous harm to the common good of the country'.[18]

Much discussion has centred around this parenthesis. It suggests that in extreme circumstances revolution might be justified (in line with 'just war' theory) but it does not explicitly say so, and could hardly be invoked to encourage people to use violent means to overcome injustice. One can only say that such resistance is not necessarily ruled out. In 1979 at the time of the final insurrection against the Somoza dictatorship in Nicaragua, people quoted this paragraph to justify their participation in the overthrow of the cruel family dynasty which had ruled their country since the 1930s. It was cited too at the time of the non-violent overthrow of the Marcos dictatorship in the Philippines.

Populorum Progressio presses for urgent change: 'We must make haste. Too many people are suffering, others stand still or move backwards; and the gap between them is widening.'[19] 'The present state of affairs must be confronted boldly . . . Continuing development calls for bold innovations that will work profound changes.'[20] But how? Various means are suggested: more international aid,[21] limits on competitive trading,[22] an international development plan,[23] the establishment of an effective world authority.[24] But how will all this come about?

In reality there are only two options: consensus – which depends on the willing agreement of all parties based on good will and a shared vision of the common good; and confrontation – which assumes those with power will only relinquish it under pressure.

In the optimistic climate of the late 1960s (which also produced the Pearson Report to the UN with its expectations of development towards the year 2000 supported by the world's wealthy nations contributing 0.7% of GNP in aid to the developing nations) Paul VI assumed a consensus model, convinced that the world was 'anxious to establish closer ties of brotherhood' and 'a more human way of life'.[25] If concessions are not made they may be forced on the rich and powerful but violence and revolution lie in that direction. The reality, of course, is that the aid policies of the rich nations have in general moved away from the 0.7% target rather than towards it. More significantly, what is entirely absent from *Populorum Progressio* is any suggestion that the poor should mobilize themselves politically in (non-violent) action for change.

Who then are the agents for change? *Populorum Progressio* provides responses at different levels. First, everyone is entitled to be shapers of their own destiny[26] and, ultimately, development is something people have to do for themselves – hence the importance of education and literacy.[27] Secondly, there must be a more central role for those who have power and influence – i.e. rich nations, international agencies (especially the UN), statesmen, journalists, educators, learned people. Thirdly, there is a key role within the Third World for students sent for higher education in developed countries and for experts and development workers from the rich countries. Finally, the church itself must make a vital contribution with its vision of 'integral human development' – the idea that true development must encompass the development of the whole person and every person.[28]

Thus according to *Populorum Progressio* the agents of change are those with wealth, power and influence. This fits in with the consensus model: the changes should be brought about by those 'at the top' – they must agree and then mould others. It is a model which continues to dominate much well-intentioned thinking. The campaign for a Millennium Jubilee[29] as we prepare for the year 2000 is based on the same approach. Third World Debt will be eased by a process of redistribution to iron out the inequalities which have arisen. But it will be initiated by those at the top. Today we have to think not just whether, realistically, this is likely to happen but also whether it ever could under such a model.

For a 'people-power' model to work there would have to be more emphasis on the political and critical awareness that could come from education and literacy (the 'conscientization' process championed by the Brazilian educationalist Paulo Freire). *Populorum Progressio* omits this, or any reference to the political options that go with adult education programmes. Likewise the theological insight that the poor are specially called by God to transform society had still to become prominent. Nonetheless *Populorum Progressio* represented a watershed. It is a landmark text – prophetic but not rash, measured but not bland, coherent, consistent, and authoritative, and it stands powerfully on its own. It has inspired, encouraged and brought great hope to countless thousands in North and South alike. It became a charter for the overseas aid agency of the Catholic Church in England and Wales, CAFOD, and many other agencies founded in the church to promote human development.

Populorum Progressio brought to the heart of Catholic Social Teaching a number of crucial new components. The concept of 'integral human development' brought to the centre of debate the notion that all must benefit from development. Structural economic injustice was identified and condemned. A new more holistic rationale was given to overseas development aid in general and to development agencies like CAFOD and promoters of fair trade like Traidcraft. There was a new imperative for action in sharing wealth and securing fair trade. Most of all there was Paul VI's realization that 'development is the new name for peace'.

From economics to politics

In July 1968 the encyclical *Humanae Vitae* dealing with birth control was published. Thereafter it was this teaching (and no other) which was linked with Paul VI's name in the popular and public perception. Yet only three years later he published another seminal document, *Octagesima Adveniens*. As its name suggests this letter marks the eightieth anniversary of *Rerum Novarum*, Leo XIII's encyclical of 1891, from which time in Catholic Social Teaching seems to be measured. It comes just four years after *Populorum Progressio*, but the focus has now shifted from economics and development to politics.

After the treatment meted out to *Humanae Vitae* Paul VI issued no more encyclicals and preferred other styles of document. So although *Octagesima Adveniens* was clearly meant to be in the main tradition of Catholic Social Teaching it was published as an apostolic letter, addressed to the President of the Council for the Laity and of the Pontifical Commission for Justice and Peace, Cardinal Maurice Roy. It was also an affirmation of these new post-Vatican II bodies which were – and still are – low in the curial hierarchy of prestige.

The spirit of *Octagesima Adveniens* derived from the conclusions of the second meeting of CELAM, the Council of Latin American Bishops, which had taken place in Medellín, Colombia some three years earlier (September/October 1968). Paul VI had been profoundly affected by what was going on in Latin America, especially through attending the Medellín meeting. At Medellín the bishops applied the teaching of the council and *Populorum Progressio* to the situation in Latin America. But where *Populorum Progressio* spoke of development, the Medellín conclusion talked of 'liberation' and took up the idea of conscientization and the transfer of power to the poor through literacy and education. The conference became a turning point in the life of the Latin American church – providing the fundamental basis for those working for radical renewal and being, in effect, the baptism of the theology of liberation.

What is most distinctive about *Octagesima Adveniens* is its modesty: Pope Paul no longer seeks to give one teaching to cover all situations (as his predecessors had done) but admits that popes cannot be abreast of the situation in all parts of the world.[30] The communities, the people on the ground, must analyse their own situation and shed light on it from studying the gospel. Hence subsidiarity is being invoked with Cardijn's see–judge–act pastoral cycle[31] as a methodology. In the midst of profound changes taking place in society, light needs to be shed on contemporary situations by eternal truths. Each local church has a responsibility to discern and to act. The major challenges identified by Paul VI as urgent are:

- urbanization – the result of a flight from the land and an industrial growth which make people slaves to 'things'; slums, unemployment, and the emergence of the 'megalopolis' or giant city such as Calcutta, Mexico City, Sao Paulo or Manila: the city needs to be humanized;[32]
- young people who are opting out and questioning authority;[33]
- the oppression of women – a charter is needed which ends discrimination and establishes equal rights to participate in political, social, economic and cultural life;[34]
- the rights of workers – the right to work is fundamental; unions should be recognized and legitimate aspirations met, but limits must be set;[35]
- the 'new poor' – the handicapped and disabled, the old, those on the fringes of society;[36]
- those discriminated against on grounds of race, origin, colour, sex, culture or religion;[37]
- emigrant workers – everything should be done to facilitate their integration with their host society;[38]

- population growth – there must be investment in employment and education; neo–Malthusian responses for population control are not the solution;[39]
- the communications media may have negative as well as positive potential;[40]
- the environment – ill-considered exploitation of nature brings risk of degradation.[41]

This is more a list of areas of concern rather than the more profound analysis of *Populorum Progressio*. But in these areas Paul VI acknowledges:

> Ever finer discernment is needed, in order to strike at the root of newly arising situations of injustice and to establish progressively a justice which will be less and less imperfect[42] . . . It is everyone's duty . . . to work with energy for the establishment of universal brotherhood, the indispensable basis for authentic justice and the condition for enduring peace[43] . . . The Christian must turn to these new perceptions in order to take on responsibility, together with everyone else, for a destiny which from now on is shared by all.[44]

The letter moves into a treatise on politics and ideologies: 'Economic activity is necessary and . . . can give rise to dialogue and cooperation. Yet it runs the risk of unduly absorbing human energies and limiting people's freedom. This is why the need is felt to pass from economics to politics . . . The ultimate decision rests with political power.'[45] This is the meat of the document. *Octagesima Adveniens* is no longer so focussed (as *Populorum Progressio* was) on development as if it were an overall process in which all are engaged and where some at an early stage have simply to work our their problems. *Octagesima Adveniens* disengages from this idealized 'development' and questions the omnipresent ideology of 'progress':

> What is the meaning of this never-ending, breathless pursuit of a progress that always eludes one just when one believes one has

conquered it sufficiently in order to enjoy it in peace? . . . The quality and the truth of human relations . . . are no less significant and important for the future of society than the quality and variety of the goods produced and consumed.[46]

The fact is that some remain poor, not simply because they have not yet developed themselves, but because they have been prevented from developing by others. The response to this, Medellín had insisted, must be 'liberation' rather than 'development'; Paul VI was reluctant to use this word, but he is concerned in *Octagesima Adveniens* with the same issues.

The advance in *Octagesima Adveniens* is not so much in recognizing that the remedies to socio-economic problems lie in the political area (earlier popes had seen this) but in consciously addressing some of the political problems involved in choosing and implementing an equitable order in society. So Paul VI calls for change in the relations between nations at the level of structures and models of growth[47] and expresses concern about the potential for abuse and domination from the uncontrolled power of multinational companies.[48] The excessive concentration of means and powers already condemned by Pope Pius XI in 1931 here takes on a new and very real image. To exercise this control over our economic activity in practice *Octagesima Adveniens* calls for the devising of new forms of democracy in a way that involves everybody in shared responsibility,[49] though Paul VI does not say much about how this can come about.

Economic questions reduce to political, but politics is not an ultimate either. The Christian can adhere neither to Marxist ideology (with its atheistic materialism, its dialectic of violence, and its denial of all transcendence to human beings) nor to the ideology of 'liberal capitalism' (which withdraws every limitation on individual freedom through the exclusive seeking of interest and power). Both must go against a Christian's faith and concept of humanity.[50] Yet Paul VI discerns positive elements in historical movements as distinct from the ideologies from which they spring.[51] Christians might in some circumstances be entitled to play a part in socialist movements though they are warned of the great danger of idealizing socialism and being misled by purely abstract and theoretical distinctions about a just society, the historical movement and the ideology. In the face of 'widely varying situations' he concludes it is difficult for him to give 'a unified message . . . which has universal validity'.[52] Hence Christians in Latin America might be entitled to collaborate far more closely with socialist movements than would be appropriate in Europe or North America. The caution of *Octagesima Adveniens* was not a rejection of Medellín, which was a discernment of the signs of the times at the regional level of which Paul VI approved. Rather it was a warning against those outside Latin America generalizing from Medellín, without going through the same kind of process. But in insisting that solutions to social problems have to be worked out in the light of local cultures and socio-political systems, *Octagesima Adveniens* goes further than previous papal or conciliar documents.

It does not, though, move beyond the consensus model of *Populorum Progressio*: it does not call for a conscientization, as Medellín did, putting the poor in the driving seat, demanding change. It insists on 'a preferential respect for the poor and the special situation they have in society'[53] and 'a renewed education in solidarity'.[54] But with such a movement into politics Pope Paul does not seem to go far enough. How are the poor expected to take responsibility for their lives when, for example, in dealing with unions, Pope Paul insists that they should not become involved in matters that are 'directly political'[55] which would be trespassing on the territory of political parties?

Octagesima Adveniens still does not face up to the major issue of confrontation. Paul VI acknowledges the need for political action. But he has in mind a high ideal involving political debate and political parties – a system that has worked since World War II in the West. But the presuppositions for such a model are not present everywhere. What the intervening years have shown is that it is no longer realistic to think political struggles can be confined to a limited sphere where 'the political game' is played according to the rules. Catholic Social Teaching needs to face up to a more radical confrontation in society. The letter ends with a fresh, insistent call for action from everyone and in a poignant paragraph, more relevant than ever in the church today, Paul VI concludes:

> From Christians who at first sight seem to be in opposition as a result of starting from different options the church asks an effort at mutual understanding of others' position and motives; a loyal examination of own behaviour will suggest to each an attitude of more profound charity which while recognising the differences believes nonetheless in the possibility of convergence and unity.[56]

These words could easily have inspired Cardinal Bernardin of Chicago and fellow United States' bishops in their recent common ground project[57] which seeks to heal the breaches and faction fighting in the North American church.

Development or liberation?

Vatican II gave rise to synods in Rome every two years with representatives of bishops' conferences from around the world. The third synod met in the autumn of 1971 (only a few months after the publication of *Octagesima Adveniens*) to discuss two matters, the priesthood and justice in the world. The preparatory work was done by the Pontifical Commission for Justice and Peace which had been established by Paul VI in 1967. This was the first synod to involve lay people like the small-is-beautiful economist Barbara Ward and to consult lay people in advance through national Justice and Peace Commissions. It illustrated the powerful influence of Third World leadership in the church. Latin American bishops, fresh from implementing the Medellín directives, were a particular source of inspiration.

The document produced at the close of the synod, *Justice in the World*, generated much discussion and controversy. As a result justice and liberation came up for discussion again at the next synod in 1974. Synods were meant to give advice to the pope, not to be a 'mini-councils'. At the conclusion of this synod the President therefore suggested a simpler procedure for subsequent synods. Strictly speaking, *Justice in the World*, as the product of a synod, has lower status than an encyclical, but it is generally regarded as being part of the main corpus of Catholic Social Teaching. Papers produced after all synods since have been papal documents.

Justice in the World is more outspoken than *Populorum Progressio* about the structural injustice involved in past imperialism, which has resulted in a 'new form of colonialism in which the developing nations will be the victims of the interplay of international economic forces'.[58] This danger can be avoided only by 'liberation' – the use of the word is an advance on *Octagesima Adveniens*. But, unlike Medellín, *Justice in the World* speaks of 'liberation through development'. In the wake of ten years of the US Alliance for Progress, ten years of American-backed modernization for Latin America, 'development' had become associated for many in the Third World with the imposition of a Western model of economic growth that widened the gap between rich and poor. To them 'development' was a suspect word – often referred to with a sneer as 'developmentalism'. But elsewhere, particularly in Africa, 'development' was still a positive word. 'Liberation through development' was therefore an attempt to take account of different situations, but the bishops were well enough aware that overcoming poverty by economic growth alone was a vain hope.[59] The manifold reasons for the failure are listed: rapid population growth, rural stagnation, lack of land reform, migration to the cities, costly industry – and all these are not so much in spite of economic growth and modernization but in part because of it.

'These stifling oppressions constantly give rise to great numbers of "marginal" persons, ill-fed, inhumanly housed, illiterate and deprived of political power as well as of the suitable means of acquiring responsibility and moral dignity',[60] the document said. This so-called development has actually created a whole category of marginalized people. 'Furthermore, such is the demand for resources and energy by the richer nations, whether capitalist or socialist, and such are the effects of dumping by them in the atmosphere and the sea that irreparable damage would be done to the essential elements of life on earth, such as air and water, if their high rates of consumption and pollution, which are constantly on the increase, were extended to the whole of mankind.'[61]

These two paragraphs completely demolished the myth of simple economic development on which rich and poor had lived for a generation. There are severe limits to this kind of growth (as we have appreciated more fully since 1971). So-called development is available to only a limited number of countries, leaving less for others. Despite the spectacular growth in the Asian 'tiger economies' such as Singapore, Hong Kong and Korea, much of the Third World has slumped into a decline which makes the very concept of 'development' seem a poor joke. Most poor countries need a type of development that is not modelled on that of the richer countries: both rich and poor need a model of *sustainable* development.

At the heart of the world's structural injustices lies the lack of participation by people in determining their own destiny. On the other hand 'the influence of the new industrial and technological order favours the concentration of wealth, power and decision-making in the hands of a small public or private controlling group'.[62] The result is that masses of people are marginalized – i.e. not simply deprived economically, but deprived of the political power to change their situation. Action, the document says, is needed directed at these 'voiceless victims of injustice'.[63]

This amounts to a definite option in favour of the powerless and oppressed and *Justice in the World* goes beyond *Octagesima Adveniens* in a way that is reminiscent of the Medellín document. It then lists the various victims of injustice – migrants, refugees, political prisoners, campesinos etc. although, again, it does not spell out precisely what 'an option for the voiceless' would mean. *Justice in the World* encourages poor *nations* to take their future into their own hands,[64] but nothing clear is said to the marginalized people *within* any given society. Again the issue of confrontation (especially between rich and poor classes in society) seems to be evaded. How a Christian should act is posed in over-simplified terms[65] – the choice is between conflict and non-violence (and love). This does not do justice to the importance of non-violent confrontation which aims at establishing more equal conditions for dialogue.

In a section on 'Education for Justice' the document speaks of awakening a critical sense and making consciences aware of actual injustices as a step in the process of transforming the world. Such an education would help people resist manipulation by the media and political forces – 'conscientization' is evidently endorsed here – and enable them to determine their own destiny and bring about communities that are truly human.[66] There is some argument over whether this education is for the rich, for the poor, or both. Perhaps the document is ambiguous, but I favour both. For the rich, then, the assumption remains (as in *Populorum Progressio*) that the change will come from the top, which is the rationale for much of our First World development education activities. But for the poor, some measure of confrontation seems inevitable – an issue which Catholic Social Teaching has yet to face up to. There is no doubt that the synod wanted to show special concern for the poor. What remains in doubt is how all this is to take place.

Justice within the church

Justice in the World is strikingly new and encouraging in the way it deals with the practice of justice within the church: 'While the Church is bound to give witness to justice, she recognizes that any-one who ventures to speak to people about justice must first be just in their eyes. Hence we must undertake an examination of the modes of acting and of the possessions and lifestyle found within the Church herself.'[67]

Justice in the World goes on to mention ways in which the rights of people within the church have to be respected (for example over wages, juridical rights, participation in decision-making). Special mention is made of the rights of women (lay and religious) and of the laity in general. This support for the most vulnerable in the church gives credibility to what is said about the marginalized in society.

This section also addresses the image of the church: 'If the church appears to be among the rich and powerful of this world its credibility is diminished.'[68] The lifestyles of all must be scrutinized – bishops, priests, religious and lay people – they must be judged not simply in terms of efficiency but to see whether they help or hinder the Church in its proclamation and witness of the gospel to the poor.[69] This is a small but important part of *Justice in the World*, sketching out a scriptural theology linking poverty with justice. 'God reveals himself to us as the liberator of the oppressed and the defender of the poor.'[70] 'In his preaching Christ proclaimed the fatherhood of God towards all and the intervention of God's justice on behalf of the needy and the oppressed (Luke 6. 21–23).'[71] Wanting to repudiate the kind of dualism which would see Christianity as 'spiritual' and other worldly, *Justice in the World* insists that the 'present situation of the world, seen in the light of faith, calls us back to the very essence of the Christian message'. The gospel calls Christians to dedicate themselves to human liberation even in this world,[72] witnessing to the demand for love and justice.[73]

The passage which best sums up this theology is the most quoted part of *Justice in the World*. It has made this document famous and controversial:

> Action on behalf of justice and participation in the transforma-
> tion of the world fully appear to us as a constitutive dimension
> of the preaching of the Gospel, or, in other words, of the
> Church's mission for the redemption of the human race and its
> liberation from every oppressive situation.[74]

The full significance of this statement seems only to have emerged later. Controversy focussed on the word 'constitutive': it implied that action for justice could never be seen as incidental but rather that it was part of what 'constituted' the gospel. Justice, thus, has to be given a central place, and not be displaced in favour of more 'spiritual' or 'religious' matters. The statement has therefore come under attack from some church leaders and theologians who see the evangelizing mission of the church as primarily 'spiritual'. They would prefer the word 'integral' to 'constitutive', implying that action for justice is not absolutely essential to the life of the church but pertains only to its fullness.

This argument is really about a more fundamental disagreement about the appropriate attitude of a church faced with major injustice in society. Should it take an overtly political stand and encourage active resistance by those who are oppressed? Or should the church keep out of politics and stick to more spiritualized values?

Many who were worried about liberation theology and the politicization of the church were those who wished to minimize the importance of the synod of bishops, seeing it as having a merely consultative role. A proper discussion of the question had to wait till the next synod – in Rome in 1974.

Our debt to *Justice in the World* goes beyond the crucial acknowledgment that action for justice is a 'constitutive' dimension of preaching the gospel. It brought the relationship between 'domination' and 'liberation' into the official church vocabulary. It provided a valuable critique of the wide variety of activity which sheltered, beyond criticism, under the umbrella of so-called development. It emphasized the importance of people shaking off fatalism and taking their future into their own hands. It brought lifestyle, development education and advocacy to the heart of the justice agenda. And action for justice being given flesh in the life of local churches through Justice and Peace Commissions and groups. It was a major contribution to the impressive legacy of the church's century of social teaching.

Evangelism or evangelization?

The fourth synod met in Rome for a month in the Autumn of 1974 with the theme of 'Evangelization in the Modern World'. It produced exciting discussions but no final document. The preparatory text was drawn up by Cardinal Karol Wojtyla (later to become Pope John Paul II) and disappointed the Latin Americans: the 'signs of the times' approach was replaced by the more traditional method of deduction from natural law. Pastoral experience was accounted as only of secondary value. The synod, with Africans providing challenges to the wider church, failed to agree on a final document and handed two drafts over to the pope. Procedurally, this was a victory for those playing down the importance of synods in the life of the church – establishing a precedent followed by later synods. But it ensured time for deeper discernment. In giving Paul VI a thesis and an antithesis, so to speak, he was prompted to come up with a brilliant synthesis.

Evangelii Nuntiandi (an Apostolic Exhortation) was published on 8 December 1975 (the tenth anniversary of the end of Vatican II). It is a document of exceptional merit, a major literary work, the fruit of mature reflection on a muddled and indecisive synod. The style is distinctive: at once synodal and papal and therefore deeply collegial. It links salvation and the proclamation of the gospel with human liberation in the broadest sense – including culture as well as economics and politics. At the heart of the document's vision is 'the kingdom'. *Evangelii Nuntiandi* is clear on this important issue and quite explicit:

> As an evangeliser, Christ first of all proclaims a kingdom, the kingdom of God; and this is so important that, by comparison, everything else becomes 'the rest', which is 'given in addition'. Only the kingdom therefore is absolute and it makes everything else relative.[75]

Even the church, then, is not an end in itself but a community of believers who 'gather together in Jesus' name in order to seek together the kingdom, build it up and live it'.[76] This involves not just religious or 'churchy' activities but, for example, working to overcome oppressive structures in society. Here a major step is taken in justifying justice as a constitutive element of evangelization.[77]

Support is also provided in this respect from the way *Evangelii Nuntiandi* speaks of evangelization: 'Above all the Gospel must be proclaimed by witness . . . which involves presence, sharing, solidarity, and which is an essential element, and generally the first one, in evangelization.'[78] 'Nevertheless this always remains insufficient, because even the finest witness will prove ineffective in the long run if it is not explained, justified and made explicit by a clear and unequivocal proclamation of the Lord Jesus.'[79] Whereas Vatican II gave priority to verbal preaching, we have here by contrast equal insistence on both word and witness. Witness without words remains ambiguous; words without witness lack credibility. An older theology which saw worldly activity as just a preparation for the gospel is rejected by Paul VI.

There is an important development too in thinking on the important concept of 'liberation'. As we have seen, *Gaudium et Spes* and *Populorum Progressio* used 'development' as a key word. By contrast Medellín focussed rather on 'liberation' but *Octagesima Adveniens* was cautious about the notion. Then *Justice in the World* deemed it as relevant for the church, but the 1974 synod had talked about 'liberation' a lot. In *Evangelii Nuntiandi*, therefore, Paul VI set out to provide a thorough theological analysis of the concept, rooting it in the gospel.

As the kernel and centre of his good news, Christ proclaims salvation, this great gift of God which is liberation from everything that oppresses human beings but which is above all liberation from sin and the evil one, in the joy of knowing God and being known by him, of seeing him, and of being given over to him.[80]

Here Paul VI clearly gives a theological respectability to the notion of 'liberation', taking the meaning well beyond the limits of politics and economics as a way of explaining the more primordial 'salvation'. Again action for justice can be seen as a constitutive element within this wider vision of evangelization. Liberation from various forms of oppression is part of the Good News of Jesus (i.e. of evangelization) – provided it comes as the gift of God (for there could be political liberation of a particular sort that was contrary to the will of God). The document's most quoted sentence says:

> The Church has the duty to proclaim the liberation of millions of human beings, the duty of assisting the birth of this liberation, giving witness to it, of ensuring that it is complete. This is not foreign to evangelization.[81]

The integral vision presented of human salvation involves a beginning in this life but a fulfilment in eternity. 'Evangelization therefore also includes the preaching of hope in the promises made by God in the new covenant in Jesus Christ, the preaching of God's love for all . . . which is the kernel of the Gospel.'[82] We are dealing with a salvation that is both immanent and transcendent – relating to earthly 'desires, hopes, affairs and struggles' but also 'exceeding all these limits'.[83]

Pope Paul uses the word 'liberation' freely, but is anxious to correct possible misunderstandings. Liberation cannot be reduced. The liberation proclaimed by Christ 'cannot be limited to any restricted sphere whether it be economic, political, social or cultural. It must rather take account of the whole human person in all its aspects, including openness to the Absolute that is God.'[84] In other words, 'integral human development' remains the goal and it should not be sold short.

Liberation cannot be merely political. What the church has to offer is not a specific political or social programme but rather an integral vision of what it means to be human. If the more transcendent aspects are ignored then Christianity would have nothing to add beyond what politics can offer. Paul VI was clearly worried that some in Latin America might interpret the church's commitment to liberation as giving support to Marxist ideology. Equally Christianity might also be hijacked or harnessed to right-wing movements.

Liberation is not synonymous with salvation. 'The Church sees the links between human liberation and salvation in Jesus Christ, but does not consider the two to be identical.'[85] The achievement of political liberation may truly be seen as a salvific event (as was the Exodus for the Jewish people) but such liberation does not constitute the coming of the kingdom: all temporal liberation contains within it the seeds of failure and these tend to grow and create a widening gap from the ideal salvation being reached for. Some notions of liberation are simply incompatible with the Christian view of the human person. The despair that enveloped some of those Christians who had committed themselves to liberation movements in Latin America when those movements failed was a tragic confirmation that some at least had made too facile an identification between God's kingdom and a particular political project. In the early chapters of the Acts of the Apostles there is the reminder that the kingdom will come in God's time. This is Paul VI's warning.

The most obvious objection to 'liberation' was that it could be used to justify violent rebellion against unjust regimes. For this reason some church leaders were urging the Vatican to condemn liberation theology. As we have seen Paul VI clarifies what 'liberation' means for Christians and then criticizes misinterpretations. He dissociates the church unequivocally from violence: it is uncontrollable; it provokes further violence and gives rise to new forms of oppression, more serious than before. 'We exhort you not to place your trust in violence and revolution: that is contrary to the Christian spirit, and it can also delay instead of advancing that social uplifting to which you lawfully aspire,'[86] he says, quoting his own address in Colombia. Sudden or violent changes are illusory and are of their nature ineffective. Paul VI does not even refer to the exceptional circumstances which might justify violence, as he did in *Populorum Progressio*. But here in *Evangelii Nuntiandi* he is presenting a pastoral inspiration rather than a comprehensive statement covering everything.

Liberation is not just about changing structures. Such a change alone is not sufficient for human liberation. What is needed is 'a conversion of the hearts and minds of those who live under these systems and of those who have control of the system'.[87]

But attentions to the systems and structures which influence and constrain human behaviour is crucial. In one of the most enlightening passages in all Catholic Social Teaching, Paul VI explores what the task of the church in the world really is. The various strata of the human race are to be transformed by the power of the Good News:

> For the Church it is a question not only of preaching the Gospel in ever wider geographic areas or to ever greater numbers of people, but also of affecting, and as it were upsetting, through the power of the Gospel, humankind's criteria of judgement, determining values, points of interest, lines of thought, sources of inspiration and models of life, which are in contrast with the word of God and the plan of salvation.[88]

> What matters is to evangelise people's culture and cultures (not in any purely decorative way as it were by applying a thin veneer, but in a vital way, in depth and right to their very roots) . . . the Gospel and evangelization can penetrate all cultures while being neither subordinate to any of them nor the monopoly of any.[89]

The gospel, then, poses a challenge to every culture, calling for a basic transformation in the traditions, the thought-pattern and the value systems of each culture.

The pope suggests the most important structures in our world are our patterns of thinking and feeling and valuing.[90] Although deeply personal, in many respects these transcend the individual and are part of the 'strata' of the human race that are to be evangelized and transformed. The point is that people can be oppressed by structures of the mind (for example by distorted value systems or inherited prejudices) and there is need here of liberation. Such a change is essential because 'even the best structures and the most wisely planned systems soon become dehumanized if the inhuman tendencies of people's hearts are not healed'.

Evangelii Nuntiandi was Paul VI's crowning achievement. The genius of the document provided major inspiration to a generation – embodied perhaps most vividly in the witness of Oscar Romero, the murdered Archbishop of San Salvador, who regarded it as the basis of his teaching and pastoral practice. Countless other pastoral workers have found affirmation and hope there too.

In the letter Paul VI is essentially giving 'confirmation' to a liberation theology 'baptized' at Medellín which does not advocate or legitimate violence. It would need to wait for the encyclical letter of Pope John Paul II, *Sollicitudo Rei Socialis*, in 1987 for its 'communion' with the whole church.[91]

With *Evangelii Nuntiandi* we have 'action for justice' and 'liberation for the poor' together with 'transformation of the world' truly written into the genetic code of evangelization. It is no wonder that 'evangelism' and 'evangelization' are quite distinct and why this decade, supposedly dedicated simultaneously to both of them, has been a mixture and a mess in Britain.

It is not difficult to understand why Paul VI referred to *Evangelii Nuntiandi* as his 'spiritual testament'. Together with his *Populorum Progressio* and *Octagesima Adveniens* and the 1971 synod document *Justice in the World* it is part of a major development of Catholic social thought, setting in place the components of an overriding ecclesial commitment to the poor of the world. The stage was set for Pope John Paul II to articulate explicitly the concept as 'the preferential option for the poor' which would powerfully hold together the whole rich tapestry of Catholic Social Teaching through its century-long evolution.

4

People before Profit: The Early Social Doctrine of John Paul II

Ian Linden

The election of Cardinal Karol Wojtyla, Archbishop of Cracow, as Pope John Paul II on 16 October 1978 ended a long, unbroken line of Italian popes. It brought to the conduct and thinking of the papacy a significantly different set of experiences compared to those of his predecessors, and a historical consciousness rooted in the troubled history of Poland and its church. It brought to the evolution of Catholic Social Teaching the pre-occupations that stemmed from this history, and from a tightly knit hierarchical church that had formed a cultural and spiritual laager, first against the Nazis, and then against bureaucratic communism.

Likewise the new pope was heir to different philosophical influences. He had been in post-war Rome at a time when the church's traditional philosophical tradition – known as Thomist after St Thomas Aquinas who synthesized the thought of Aristotle and St Augustine – was under intense debate, and, when he returned as doctor of divinity to the Jagiellonian University in Cracow, it was on the personalist philosophy of Emmanuel Mounier that he focussed under the influence of his friend, the Polish intellectual, Jerzy Turowicz. Personalism was a philosophy which rejected the split between mind and body which had dominated Western thinking since Descartes; instead it celebrated the unity of the individual based on the notion that it is through creative action that human beings realize their potential. The future pope's studies and writing turned to the personalist thought of the German philosopher, Max Scheler, in their relation to

Christian ethics. He was later to teach philosophy and ethics at the fiercely independent Catholic university of Lublin where as a student chaplain he proved open to the intellectual challenge of Marxist-Christian dialogue. Rome thus had a new pope who surprisingly salted his Thomism with a strong helping of personalism and a detailed knowledge of Marxism, a man from an unhappy personal family background who saw the church as his family, a staunch Polish nationalist whose job description asked of him a universal leadership.

It was perhaps God's little joke that within three months of a philosopher pope from Middle Europe taking up office, he was projected into the conflicts of another continent with which he was unlikely to have natural sympathy or immediate, intuitive understanding. The Latin American Bishops Conference at Puebla in Mexico was the forum for a titanic struggle. On the one side stood those who wanted to implement the 'option for the poor' which had been first outlined at the previous great 1968 conference in Medellín. On the other were arch-conservatives who wanted to 'purify' the church from the contamination of the radical social action on behalf of the poor which Medellín had endorsed.

In the event the new pope performed a credible diplomatic balancing act denouncing those who would distort the nature of Christ by turning him into a mere political agent, while endorsing the church's 'preferential option for the poor'. He would not have felt fully at home in the world of those who wanted to 're-spiritualize' the church. But nor would he have been content in that of those militant Catholic activists who borrowed freely, and sometimes uncritically, from Marxist thought. His encounter with poverty in Mexico and, later in Brazil, may well account for the strong, emotional language used in his first encyclical about the failure of development and the growth of destitution on a global scale. 'There are babies dying of hunger under their mothers' eyes . . . entire areas of poverty, shortage and underdevelopment . . . their numbers reach tens, even hundreds of millions,' he was later to write in *Dives in Misericordia* published in November 1980.

The theology of pessimism

The initial output of the pope and his Polish advisers was prodigious. In quick succession they wrote three new major pastoral letters – *Redemptor Hominis* (1979), *Dives in Misericordia* (1980) and *Laborem Exercens* (1981). John Paul II's early social thought deals in one way or another with an awesome question –: what it means to be human. And his answer is that it is essentially to be 'a person in community'. Human potential is realized through action, work and by acting in solidarity with others. This personalist approach means that 'the primary route that the Church must pursue in fulfilling her mission'[1] is the human person, because the mystery of the human person is only revealed in God. This vision does away with the dualism between spiritual and material that had dogged Christian thought since the eighteenth. century. In its place it proposes an 'integral human-ism'.[2] But it also takes the church further away from any 'natural' understanding of what it meant to be human that might easily be shared with non-believers; a Christian anthropology could only start with and in Christ.

Nonetheless, as the new pope returned to Europe on the eve of what the historian Eric Hobsbawn calls 'the second Cold War', his central message that people always had precedence over the economy could not have been more pertinent. The two super-powers were locked in an economic struggle focussed on arma-ments production that was willing to – and did in different ways – sacrifice people before the altar of their economies. His championing of the rights of workers and denunciation of paths of development and exploitation that were ultimately destructive of the human person were based on far more than philosophical first principles.

Redemptor Hominis in 1979 was in some sense the new pope's mission and vision statement, a theological setting out of his stall that is, at times, mystical and is profoundly christocentric – underlining that saving knowledge of God and the fullness of human potential comes in his revelation in Christ. It immediately illustrated that the approach taken by Catholic social teaching and found in the letters of Pope John and Pope Paul had undergone a significant change of direction. Concrete analysis of the human condition, rooted in history, sociology, economics or politics, had never previously been well-elaborated in papal encyclicals. Nonetheless it had been slowly developing over time. Henceforth, under John Paul II, it was to stay rudimentary.

The mood of this thinking was distinctive too. It was very different from Pope John's 1960s optimism. It was deeply pessimistic. In a sense the pessimism was programmed into the philosophical position. For the progress produced by men and women throughout history would always stand as a threat against John Paul's 'Transcendent Man'. In *Redemptor Hominis* he faithfully re-iterates Pope Paul VI's *Populorum Progressio* and in it includes a trenchant critique of 'economic progress'.

Progress, he said, has become to many an end in itself which subordinates 'the whole of human existence to its partial demands, suffocating man, breaking up society, and ending by entangling itself in its own tensions and excesses'.[3] The result is that instead of being 'stewards' of creation, people become despoilers and polluters. He sees the clearest instance of this in atomic weapons and the abuse of power by governments.[4] The temptation to war was, he told the United Nations in September 1979, 'not so much in the hearts of the nation, but in the inner determination of the systems that decide the history of whole societies'. The pope speaks of all this producing 'an understandable sense of disquiet, of conscious and unconscious fear and of menace',[5] or of a 'moral uneasiness'.[6]

In the end the pope believes that the idea of real human progress is inherently flawed. 'It is obvious that a fundamental defect – or rather series of defects, indeed a defective machinery – is at the root of contemporary economics and materialistic civilization which does not allow the human family to break free from such radically unjust situations.'[7] People become slaves to things. They want to have more rather than to be more, and create the consumer society. Moral and technological development are tragically out of kilter. The international economic order, since it is the ground of this misdevelopment, must also be flawed and dysfunctional. The pope sets the vast spending on the arms trade against the growing needs of the poor; the surplus wealth of one group of countries is thus connected to the destitution of others. An enormous task of transforming this situation faces the church and all people of good-will. The central virtue which will enable this to happen is solidarity, a theme he will develop more extensively at a later date.[8] 'Integral human development' is therefore a necessary correction to a 'progress' whose inner dynamic is flawed.

All this is set by the pope in the context of the Christian story of salvation history. Against the reality of flawed progress the pope sets nothing less than the Last Judgment. 'I was hungry and you gave me food . . . naked and you did not clothe me . . . in prison and you did not visit me.' The only real yardstick against which to measure progress is therefore a moral responsibility arrived at through a personal examination of conscience.[9] There could scarcely be a stronger assertion that the struggle against systemic poverty must be the central moral and spiritual pre-occupation of the church. And in this context the pope described respect for human rights and human dignity as the measure of social justice. 'The common good that authority in the state serves is brought to full realization only when all the citizens are sure of their rights.'[10] And, as he told the United Nations, 'the economic tensions with countries, and in the relationships between states . . . contain within themselves substantial elements that restrict or violate human rights'.

This sombre portrait of economic progress is only briefly lightened by the acknowledgment that many people are now awakened to global problems and working for justice. But instead of encouraging them, the encyclical merely uses this upsurge in popular movements to warn against those who nominally set out to restore justice but are in reality more motivated by 'spite, hatred and even cruelty'.[11] It is possible to become repressive in your search for justice, he says, if you are single-mindedly in pursuit of the justice of equality rather than the justice of God. What he is saying is that mercy and justice are two sides of the same coin and should not be set one against the other. But the overall impression falls sadly short of a wholehearted endorsement of work for justice and popular movements and the empowerment of people. A reference to 'class justice' and the emphasis given to religious freedom as a human right – only belatedly recognized by the church in the late 1940s – makes it very clear how much the pope's thinking here is directed to and arises from Eastern Europe. Communism sits on his thinking here like a gloomy pall. This reduces the relevance of much that he wrote to the peoples of the Third World. Often, branded communists as a pretext for persecution, their real enemy was not bureaucratic Marxism but the oppressive social and political system that generated their poverty. For this reason parts of the encyclical have implications which do not move outside the time or particular context in which they were written.

This was a pity because the initial output of the pope and his Polish advisers was both innovative and prodigious. But in each of his first three major pastoral letters – *Redemptor Hominis*, *Dives in Misericordia* and *Laborem Exercens* – the daily lives of the poor and how things were in the world, appeared essentially as a peg for an elaborate moral, philosophical and theological reflection. 'We are not dealing with "abstract" man, but the real, "concrete", "historical" man,' the pope protested. 'We are dealing with "each" man, for each one is included in the mystery of redemption.' But the text sometimes belied his protestations.

It was as if, with the new pope, Catholic social thinking had taken off, soaring away upwards and backwards, into a cloud of idealism. It was an intellectual world in which the parameters seem partially defined by a continuing, but unsignalled, dialogue with Marxism. It did not lend itself to clarity. In the hands of John Paul II, Marxist terms were used, but in a manner which entirely transformed their meaning, leaving arguments hanging in the air. So these early papal letters are not easy documents to read, understand or act on, even though the applications of his thinking on the world of work have clearer practical and political outcomes.

Work and the heart of human identity

If *Redemptor Hominis* and *Dives in Misericordia* ask the question what it is to be human, *Laborem Exercens*, which completes the trilogy and was published while the pope was recovering from an assassination attempt in September 1981, opens up the theme of work. But it does so as a profound reflection on human creativity and how this creative action is a constitutive dimension of being human. It reveals the Catholic Church as a protagonist of trade unionism, concerned at a global level with the rights of workers, and with the world of work as central to its concerns about justice, yet with an analysis that sets out to differentiate itself from Marxism.

As one in the series of anniversary publications published by previous popes, celebrating *Rerum Novarum* of 1891, the text makes differences from the writing of his predecessors particularly apparent. The style of a philosophical and theological university essay becomes more firmly entrenched, and there is little reference to previous social teaching on the subject, at least not the usual compendious citations of former encyclicals that usually serve to emphasize the continuity of the organic tradition of Catholic Social Teaching. In many ways this encyclical comes as an application of the personalist philosophy found in his book *The Acting Person*,[12] first published in Polish in 1969.

Work for John Paul II is the quintessential human activity through which men and women 'subdue the earth', thereby sharing in God's creativity. Work is thus the defining act which makes us fully human. This is, in a sense, a logical corollary of the primacy of action in the pope's philosophy. The word 'work' has such broad connotations that it virtually may be translated as 'creative human action'. It certainly does not merely mean wage labour or employment in the normal usage.[13] Such human acts take place against the horizon of an absolute truth and an ethical norm. They either comply with them – and therefore qualify to be described a genuine personal development, realization of the potential of the self in a particular culture – or they do not, and are reprehensible.

Human beings exist in the historical continuum of progress and development inheriting the work of previous generations, and will themselves produce the 'earth' of generations to come. Since work here also means intellectual work this account does not lend itself to a simplistic Marxist materialist determinism. Likewise what makes work 'work' and not adaptive animal behaviour is that a person undertakes it. It is defined by its subjective dimension and not the objective product of the work itself.[14]

If people take priority over things then, the pope wants to assert that labour must take priority over capital. But to say that baldly would run him right into ideological trouble; his words might sound dangerously close to those of Marxism which sees labour and capital as forces locked irredeemably in conflict. The pope wants to avoid the idea of class conflict at all costs. So he gets round the problem. He does so by the simple subterfuge of completely transforming the meaning of 'capital'. Marx used it, within his critical analysis of capitalism, to mean money or money invested in productive machinery for industry. By contrast the pope uses it to indicate any productive resource – from machinery to crops to the human intellect – which he then confusingly calls 'the means of production'[15] (a term which Marx also uses but in a more narrow and precise sense).

Since these means of production, nature, science and technology, are simply the inherited accretions of past generations' work, he goes on, there can be no conflict between labour and capital; the two are intermingled on the great workbench of humanity. The problem only comes, he argues when 'economism' takes over – by which he means that the spiritual and human dimensions of 'labour' are abandoned and 'labour' becomes merely a key economic factor. It is this materialism which, he says, falsely divides labour and capital in a binary opposition that neglects the primacy of the person.[16]

It is in such passages that the reader senses that Catholic social teaching may be heading up a blind alley in its determination to avoid the necessity of class conflict. He completely fails to engage with the theoretical Marxist analysis of wage labour, exploitation and the issue of the ownership of the means of production. Nor is it of much use to the majority of people in the world who have never been embroiled in the finer points of Marxist-Christian dialogue under an oppressive communist regime. It was the abject failure in the 1980s of the economic and social practice of bureaucratic communism that led to its downfall, rather than this kind of rather tortured theory coming from the Catholic Church as an intellectual refutation of Marxist philosophy and economic theory.

The fall of communism left the champions of free-market neo-liberal capitalism in the West triumphantly proclaiming that Marxism was devoid of insights, and as an economic system was a busted flush. History, they proclaimed, had ended. Yet for all that, it worried and annoyed them, that here was the Catholic Church still proposing a Christian form of socialism. In a sense, as Gregory Baum suggests in his book *The Priority of Labour: A Commentary on Laborem Exercens*,[17] they were quite right; a pre-Marxist socialism was what the church was proposing. It is difficult to see how any normal meaning of the phrase 'priority of labour' would find a comfortable home in anything other than the political tradition of socialism. Moreover the pope explicitly writes of the need for 'various adaptations in the sphere of the right to ownership of the means of production'.[18] And he later draws a useful distinction between state ownership of the means of production and what he calls their 'socialization'. The pope suggests that it is important to avoid bureaucratic centralization of power in order to ensure that each worker feels that he/she is working 'for himself'.[19] Such a distinction, found for example in the 1940s debate over nationalization of the mines in Britain, has normally only taken place within a socialist discourse.

The indirect employer

Once the subterranean skirmishes with Polish Marxism have been concluded, the encyclical gains in clarity and introduces some novel concepts. A consideration of work at a global level leads to the idea of the 'indirect employer'. This is an heuristic device to allow two opposing ideas apparently to be reconciled. On the one hand, there is the fundamental concept that human persons are morally responsible for their actions; personal moral responsibility is always the necessary corollary of freedom. On the other hand, there is the reality of 'structural injustice'.

Structures for the pope are always determined by persons, never the other way round, which would be too Marxist for him. (Liberation theologians like Gustavo Gutiérrez see the personal and the structural interacting in a many-sided process.) He starts with the question: 'how can it be that economic structures force employers to pay inhuman wages in the Third World?' He is referring here to the fact that the system forces employers to pay badly if they are to survive; pay well and their competitors undercut them so they go out of business. At first sight everyone is trapped in a system which perpetuates injustice. But the pope cannot accept that people are not to blame. To get round the problem he invents the concept of the 'indirect employer' . This covers the many different factors 'that exercise a determining influence on the shaping both of the work contract and, consequently, of just or unjust relationships in the field of human labour'.[20] Thus the direct employer in a sweatshop in China, Thailand or Hackney is co-responsible with many others who make it impossible to, say, pay a just wage or create proper health and safety conditions at work, for fear of pricing the product out of the market. And the 'indirect employer' is us – the people who benefit from the unjust situation by buying cut-price goods.

This widening of moral responsibility to those who benefit from cheap goods is an important ethical dimension of Catholic Social Teaching. It puts the consumer, the transnational corporation, the pension fund, the shareholder and the state into the moral dock. It provides a social and structural reference to the ethics of trade and commerce, and reveals far more than simply the individual as a moral agent.

So, while at first sight the notion of the 'indirect employer' may seem cumbersome, it opens up the possibility of a whole range of action on behalf of justice. The growth of ethical investment, fair trade organizations, consumer lobbies and the quest for 'social clauses' in trade agreements, all in one way or another might be understood as action at the level of the 'indirect employer'. Governments and NGOs like development agencies and churches are thus able to influence the course of development in a way that was little imagined before the 1980s.

Likewise the concept of the 'indirect employer' eases people into an understanding of what later becomes known as 'structural sin'[21] and away from the notion that only persons are bearers of sin. This clearly worries the pope and not simply because in much of Europe the confessional, where the sacrament of penance for personal sin is predominantly enacted, is fast emptying. The pope would not want to say that structures make people sinful because this has a Marxist and determinist ring to it. Yet, it is just as meaningful to emphasize that in South Africa apartheid structures made people sinful, as to say that people made sinful apartheid structures. South Africans were, of course, free to resist apartheid, and qualify for prison, just as their parents or grandparents had been free to resist the setting up of apartheid structures, and qualify for prison. Likewise everyone wishing to stay out of prison, or labour camp, compromised to some extent with the sinful structures of bureaucratic communism in Eastern Europe.

Of course, liberation theologians, like Gustavo Gutiérrez, would portray the relationship between persons and structures as interactive. For Pope John Paul II, though, it is a one way street: persons create structures, not the other way round. In the 'indirect employer' he therefore tries to 'personalize' a structure to avoid the conceptual dilemma. The implications are politically most significant. There is no need to change structures if it is, as the pope has it, a one-way street. Changing lots of hearts will do. So changing hearts becomes the business of the church. Work for social justice becomes 'politics'.

Unfortunately this is bad theology and utopian in the worst sense. Take the simple example of women workers in toy factories in Thailand and southern China. It would be quixotic to seek adequate workers' rights for them (health and safety at work, for example,) by seeking the evangelical conversion of individuals amongst the direct employers – the factory owners – or indeed, the conversion of individuals amongst the big players who are indirect employers which include the large transnational toy buyers. In reality to bring about change in the direct employers means working through negotiation and pressure on a complex group of indirect employers. That much is clear in practice. The British development agencies CIIR (the Catholic Institute for International Relations) and the World Development Movement, together with the Trades Union Congress, lobbied on this question from 1994–1997. They persuaded the international toy buyers to agree to a Code of Conduct for toy factories not by changing their hearts – though some hearts and minds might have been changed – but by benefiting from their vulnerability to public opinion, and by potential consumer pressure, to bring about structural change.

The example of the toy factories – where hundreds of women have in the past died through factory fires – reveals a general principle in work for social justice and a corresponding danger in the social teaching of Pope John Paul II. By moving away from a tradition of socio-economic and political analysis, there is a danger of over-personalizing structural sin. Every evil system is sustained by evil people but, far more, by the vast multitude of people who do not resist because they are structurally embedded in it, and who may in their very survival within it – as with that great hero of survival, the Good Soldier Schweik[22] – seem positively heroic.

Structures do have a life of their own. People who lived in communist Eastern Europe are marked by that experience in a different way from those who lived in capitalist Western Europe, Latin America or Africa. Their historical consciousness and thus, in some respects their 'informed' conscience, is similarly different.

The vision in Catholic Social Teaching that humankind has a divine destiny and therefore significance, and requires the social, political and economic means appropriate to achieving it, is perhaps nowhere more focussed than in these early encyclicals of Pope John Paul II, rooted in the Thomism of the University of Lublin. He sets out in it a Christian anthropology which has immense implications for our political systems and the type of society we seek. At the very least, the place given to creative action in this anthropology implies meaningful work as a basic human right. It might be argued that it implies that an economic system premised on a fundamental contradiction between equity and efficiency, labour and capital, full employment and other economic 'goods', like control of inflation, must be inherently flawed.

At one level the pope clearly recognizes that the dynamics of economic progress, and its contemporary structures, have a nefarious impact on the human person, and offers dire warnings. At another he seems to be saying that the development of the human person, in compliance with the 'truth' and with ethical norms, provided it be 'in Christ', can escape these consequences of being embedded in particular economies and societies. It is a conflation – or at least lack of clear indication of what is being discussed – of how things are compared with how God wants them to be, of the 'order of creation' with the 'order of redemption' or, to put it another way, of 'nature' with 'grace', that often creates a sense of confusion in these early encyclicals.

This ought not detract from the importance of this thinking. The pope's repeated personalist call to solidarity and personal responsibility for structural sin re-humanizes the social and the political by making it a moral domain. It repeatedly subjects the notion of progress to an interrogation by the lofty concept of human development. In so doing, however pessimistic its verdict, it makes 'development' the operational principle of human history, and makes of Christianity a profoundly subversive creed.

5

Structures of Sin and the Free Market: John Paul II on Capitalism

Clifford Longley

What is very impressive about Catholic Social Teaching is the way it holds together, objectively and coherently. Those who are used to a certain kind of Protestant or Anglican commentary on social affairs will be familiar with the sort of nagging private doubts as to whether what is being said truly derives 'from the gospel' or 'from the church' rather than from the private political opinions and sometimes unstated prejudices of those who wrote the document. Others, no less Christian, may bring different prejudices to bear, and therefore reach different conclusions. Which then is the true Christian view? Is it, for example, Margaret Thatcher's Christian vision of society (and a pretty ardent vision it was too) or is it the *Faith in the City* vision, a much more statist, interventionist and left-of-centre formula, that we can call an authentically Christian vision of society? We have here the makings of a quite unfruitful slanging match between two schools, each side of which regards its own vision for society as Christian, and the other vision as flawed. In Britain it is a divide not so much between the parties as within each of them. In the Labour party the real divide comes between what might be termed ethical socialism and left-wing libertarianism. In the Tory party, the line comes between social market theorists and the unlimited free marketeers, who are often in fact right-wing libertarians.

Catholic Social Teaching offers us a route to escape this total subjectivity, and discover some objective principles that can be applied to a critique of society, and to economic models within society, according to criteria which are independent of the personal prejudices and opinions of the person doing the exercise. That is to say both a Thatcherite Christian and a *Faith in the City* Christian, undertaking the task of examining society in the light of Catholic Social Teaching, ought in theory at least to arrive at the same conclusions. That will not always be the case, in practice. This is not an exact science. But asked whether Catholic Social Teaching does or does not assert the primacy of labour over capital, for instance, both Thatcherite and anti-Thatcherite would have to agree that it does.

The coherence of Catholic Social Teaching consists in the way its various principles seem to merge into and arise out of each other, almost as if each concept contains all the others. Thus if we were to lose one of the principles of Catholic Social Teaching, from some sort of theological amnesia, we could reconstruct it from the others. We would be able to say what it consisted of, so to speak, from the hole it left behind, just as we would be able to reconstruct a missing piece of a jigsaw. This is one of the reasons that Catholic Social Teaching seems to resist being organized into lists, and why it is so difficult to break it up into sub-headings. A chapter headed *The Common Good* quickly starts to invade the space reserved for the next chapter, as one cannot really take a discussion of the common good very far without also discussing, say, solidarity. Thus there is a circular quality to these related concepts – they fade into each other. They are non-linear, and not even two dimensional. Were we to try to produce a diagram, I think we would have to work in three dimensions to begin to show the various concepts in relationship to one another.

This coherence has a certain effect on the way Catholic Social Teaching is presented. Each of the major social encyclicals since *Rerum Novarum* has attempted to be a synthesis of all the teaching that has gone before. But at the same time each has tried to find, within the legacy of the earlier documents, new developments. In this chapter we are primarily concerned with the two main encyclicals of Pope John Paul II's middle period. But first it will be helpful to examine the main pillars or principles of Social Teaching as they were firmly established prior to *Sollicitudo Rei Socialis* (1987) and *Centesimus Annus* (1991).

The structures of sin

The fundamental principle of Catholic Social Teaching is that of the common good – the notion that there exist some shared or public values which transcend the rights of individuals. The common good implies a notion of subsidiarity – the idea that higher forms of government should not arrogate to themselves tasks which can be performed at a lower level. But it also fairly obviously implies a concept of solidarity – the idea that we are all responsible for one another. The key insight is that all three concepts are necessary and inter-related: without solidarity, the horizontal dimension of social structure, subsidiarity, the vertical dimension, can easily become selfish insularity. Subsidiarity and solidarity have often to be held in a necessary kind of tension.

None of these are concepts entirely new to John Paul II. The principle of the common good is present in the first social encyclical *Rerum Novarum* (1891) and the idea of solidarity is implicit in its insistence that capitalist owners have some moral responsibility for the well-being of their workers. The concept of subsidiarity was defined in *Quadragesima Anno* (1931) but it too is not a self-contained concept. It also grows from the principle of the common good, as can be seen from the 1931 definition:

> Just as it is gravely wrong to take from individuals what they can accomplish by their own initiative and industry and give it to the community, so also it is an injustice and at the same time a grave evil and disturbance of right order to assign to a greater or higher association what lesser and subordinate organizations can do. For every social activity ought of its very nature to furnish help to the members of the body social, and never destroy or absorb them. The supreme authority of the State ought, therefore, to let subordinate groups handle matters and concerns of lesser importance, which would otherwise dissipate its efforts

greatly. Thereby the State will more freely, powerfully and effectively do all those things that belong to it alone because it alone can do them: directing, watching, urging, restraining, as occasion requires and necessity demands. Therefore those in power should be sure that the more perfectly a graduated order is kept among the various associations, in observance of the principle of subsidiary function, the stronger social authority and effectiveness will be, the happier and more prosperous the condition of the State.[1]

Throughout Pius XI's teaching as elsewhere there is an implicit and intimate relationship between subsidiarity and the common good. Now consider also the concept of solidarity. It was defined by Pope John Paul in his 1987 encyclical *Sollicitudo Rei Socialis* in the following terms:

The fact that men and women in various parts of the world feel personally affected by the injustices and violations of human rights committed in distant countries, countries which perhaps they will never visit, is a further sign of a reality transformed into awareness, thus acquiring a moral connotation. It is above all a question of interdependence, sensed as a system determining relationships in the contemporary world in its economic, cultural, political and religious elements, and accepted as a moral category. When interdependence becomes recognized in this way, the correlative response as a moral and social attitude, as a 'virtue', is solidarity. This then is not a feeling of vague compassion or shallow distress at the misfortunes of so many people, both near and far. On the contrary it is a firm and persevering determination to commit oneself to the common good; that is to say, to the good of all and of each individual because we are all really responsible for all.[2]

Catholic Social Teaching in its modern phase began with *Rerum Novarum*'s examination of the question of the plight of workers in a capitalist economy. This concentration on the appalling ill treatment meted out to workers was an early example of what we later came to call the 'preferential option for the poor'. This, then, is an illustration of how the way in which the church has developed such teaching, with a specific teaching becoming applied (and gradually developed into) a more general one.

Of course workers' rights and the option for the poor are both included under the heading of solidarity, which is in turn, implicit in the concept of the common good. However, also implicit in the analysis of the plight of workers, both in the 1891 encyclical and the 1931 encyclical of Pius XI, is some sort of concept of sin beyond the purely personal. There was something about raw capitalism, both popes decided, which disposed people and society towards sin. So we see here the gradual emergence of another key doctrine – that of 'social sin', which John Paul II has defined in *Sollicitudo Rei Socialis* as structural sin or 'structures of sin'. But though it has emerged into the full light of theological truth only in the last twenty years, it was implicit all along and lurking only just below the surface in a series of documents between its seeds in *Rerum Novarum* and its full expression in *Sollicitudo Rei Socialis*.

It is there when *Gaudium et Spes*, the decree of the Second Vatican Council of 1965, declares (in a translation which predates inclusive language): 'It cannot be denied that men are often diverted from doing good and spurred towards evil by the social circumstances in which they live. The disturbances which so frequently occur in the social order result in part from the natural tensions of economic, political and social forms. But at a deeper level they flow from man's pride and selfishness, which contaminate even the social sphere. When the social structure is flawed by the consequences of sin, man, already born with a bent towards evil, finds there new inducements to sin, which cannot be overcome without strenuous efforts and the assistance of grace.' It is developed in *Salvifici Doloris* (1984) in which Pope John Paul considers 'the Christian meaning of human suffering', where we also find an element of mysticism creeping in: 'Those who share in the sufferings of Christ preserve in their own sufferings a very special particle of the infinite treasure of the world's redemption, and can share this treasure with others. The more a person is threatened by sin, the heavier the 'structures of sin' which today's world brings with it, the greater is the eloquence which human suffering possesses in itself. And the more the Church feels the need to have recourse to the value of human sufferings for the salvation of the world.' Next in *Reconciliatio et Paenitentia* (1984) John Paul II explores how structural sin uses human weakness to maintain its grasp on the world: 'Social sins are the result of the accumulation and concentration of many personal sins. It is a case of the very personal sins of those who cause or support evil or who exploit it, of those who are in a position to avoid, eliminate or at least limit certain social evils but who fail to do so out of laziness, fear or the conspiracy of silence, through secret complicity or indifference, of those who take refuge in the supposed impossibility of changing the world and also those who sidestep the effort and sacrifice required, producing spurious reasons of a higher order.'

But it is in *Sollicitudo Rei Socialis* that the concept receives its full expression. The pope begins to look at the entire world from the viewpoint of its structures. And he sees, writing at a time when positions struck during the Cold War were still in place, a world whose governance is dominated by sinful systems. Communism is perhaps his chief target, but his criticisms of capitalism are no less scathing:

It is important to note that a world which is divided into blocs, sustained by rigid ideologies, and in which instead of inter-dependence and solidarity different forms of imperialism hold sway, can only be a world subject to 'structures of sin'. The sum total of the negative factors working against a true awareness of the universal common good, and the need to further it, gives the impression of creating, in persons and institutions, an obstacle which is difficult to overcome.[3]

Some may see echoes of a Marxist analysis in this. But the pope is keen to distance himself from the notion that peoples' actions are completely determined by the systems in which they live. Structures of sin are rooted in personal sin, and thus always linked to the concrete acts of individuals who introduce these structures, consolidate them and make them difficult to remove. The sin of people and the sinful structures built into systems reinforce one another – 'and thus they grow stronger, spread, and become the source of other sins, and so influence people's behaviour'.[4] In this way there are introduced into the world 'influences and obstacles which go far beyond the actions and brief lifespan of an individual'.

A particular cause for concern for John Paul II is the impact this has on the world's poor nations. Blockages and hindrances put on the development of the Third World by the rich nations must be judged also in this light. 'Obstacles to development . . . have a moral character'.[5] He then goes on to name the chief of these obstacles as 'the all-consuming desire for profit' and 'the thirst for power, with the intention of imposing one's will upon others'.[6] These two aims are all too often pursued in the modern world 'at any price' and often are indissolubly united. He goes on:

> Obviously, not only individuals fall victim to this double attitude of sin; nations and blocs can do so too. And this favours even more the introduction of the 'structures of sin' of which I have spoken. If certain forms of modern 'imperialism' were considered in the light of these moral criteria, we would see that hidden behind certain decisions, apparently inspired only by economics or politics, are real forms of idolatry: of money, ideology, class, technology.[7]

The true nature of the evil which faces us with respect to the development of peoples is, therefore, a moral evil. 'To diagnose the evil in this way is to identify precisely, on the level of human conduct, the path to be followed in order to overcome it.'[8] It is in this context that John Paul II goes on to develop his expression of the concept of solidarity, a word which had a particular resonance with him from the name *Solidarność*, taken by the Polish trade union movement in its struggle against the communist authorities.

God requires from people clear cut attitudes which express themselves in actions or omissions toward one's neighbour, he insists. Because there is a moral dimension – as well as economic, cultural and political – to all social systems, this stresses 'above all' the interdependence of all peoples:

> When interdependence becomes recognized in this way, the correlative response as a moral and social attitude, as a 'virtue', is solidarity. This then is not a feeling of vague compassion or shallow distress at the misfortunes of so many people, both near and far. On the contrary, it is a firm and persevering determination to commit oneself to the common good; that is to say to the good of all and of each individual, because we are all really responsible for all.[9]

What hinders the development of such solidarity is the desire for profit and that thirst for power. These attitudes and 'structures of sin' are only conquered by a diametrically opposed attitude: 'a commitment to the good of one's neighbour with the readiness, in the gospel sense, to "lose oneself" for the sake of the other instead of exploiting him, and to "serve him" instead of oppressing him for one's own advantage'. What Pope John Paul is positing here is the idea that solidarity is the opposite to structural sin. It is almost as if the very concept of solidarity contains the concept of 'structures of sin' waiting to emerge like the dark side of its moon. This is another striking example of the interdependence of the various concepts which together make up Catholic Social Teaching, whereby doctrinal concepts gradually disclose more of their content and meaning without actually turning into something quite else. The earlier undeveloped doctrine and the later developed doctrine are consistent with each other and clearly related, but the later one spells out what in the earlier one is only hinted at. It is almost like dealing with ideas that had an existence of their own, and a definite shape and form that co-operate with us when we try to expand them rightly, but which resist us when we do so against their intrinsic conceptual content.

All this has something important to say to a society in which relativism increasingly holds way. We have become used to the supposition that we can invent any ideas we like, so that we think and act as if all ideas are man made and can therefore be man-unmade. It is arresting to come face to face with ideas that have a life of their own and seem to pre-exist us. We might say that the concepts at the basis of Catholic Social Teaching were discovered, in the scientific or historical sense, rather than merely invented out of nothing, as we might invent a new card game. They were there before we found them. This strange sense of pre-existence is one of the most powerful reasons for believing that the principles of Catholic Social Teaching are in fact true, and that therefore Catholic Social Teaching is not just another way for Catholics to dress up their political prejudices.

Is the free market a structure of sin?

The Tory rediscovery of free market theory in the early 1980s made it an exciting thing to be interested in political economy. A new ideology was being born, or at least an old one reborn, and its scope extended far further than theories about money supply and the causes of inflation. It was a total world view. And it was claiming for itself the commanding heights of political debate just when the contrary ideology, Marxism, seemed in retreat on all fronts. The change in emphasis provided a new challenge to the church's thinking.

'Catholic Social Teaching recognizes that market forces, when properly regulated in the name of the common good, can be an efficient mechanism for matching resources to needs in a developed society.' So said the Catholic bishops of England and Wales in *The Common Good*, a statement they prepared in October 1996 in an attempt to influence the debate in the run up to Britain's 1997 general election.

No other system has so far shown itself superior in encouraging wealth creation and hence in advancing the prosperity of the community, and enabling poverty and hardship to be more generously relieved. Centrally commanded economies, in contrast, have been seen to be inefficient, wasteful, and unresponsive to human needs. Nor have they fostered a climate of personal liberty. The existence of a wide variety of consumer choice means that individual decisions can be made according to individual wants and needs, thus respecting certain aspects of human freedom and corresponding to the principle of subsidiarity. There is no doubt, too, that competition can encourage product improvement.[10]

But, the bishops said, drawing on a synthesis of all Catholic Social Teaching to that date, a distinction has to be drawn between a technical economic method and a total ideology or world view. The church accuses free market economic theory of claiming more for itself than is warranted. In particular, an economic creed that insists the greater good of society is best served by each individual pursuing his or her own self-interest is likely to find itself encouraging individual selfishness. Thus we see that the church's social teaching explicitly rejects belief in the automatic beneficence of market forces and insists that the end result of market forces must be scrutinized and if necessary corrected in the name of natural law, social justice, human rights, and the common good. Left to themselves, it claims, market forces are just as likely to lead to evil results as to good ones.

In this the bishops draw on the writing of John Paul II and preceding popes. Sixty years earlier Pius XI articulated a similar conviction with equal force in *Quadragesimo Anno* when he declared:

The right ordering of economic life cannot be left to a free competition of forces. From this source as from a poisoned spring have originated and spread all the errors of individualistic economic teaching. Destroying through forgetfulness or ignorance the social and moral character of economic life, it held that economic life must be considered and treated as altogether free from and independent of public authority, because in the market, i.e. in the free struggle of competitors, it would have a principle of self-direction that governs it more perfectly than would the intervention of any created intellect. But free competition, while justified and certainly useful provided it is kept within certain limits, clearly cannot direct economic life – a truth which the outcome of the application in practice of the tenets of this evil individualistic spirit has more than sufficiently demonstrated.[11]

It is in this distinction between the market as a tool and as an ideology that Catholic Social Teaching has an important contribution to make to current thinking on how to make contemporary capitalism a gentler beast. All ideologies and world views have a tendency to collapse under their own weight. Far too much is claimed about their capacity to explain or prescribe; and gradually, many of those who initially believed them to be totally true begin to have doubts, as their limitations become more apparent. In the years since the fall of Margaret Thatcher it has been possible to discern, even on the right of British politics, a desire to retrieve some of the principles and values that seemed to be swept away when Thatcherism was in full flood. It is a tendency which has stood at the heart of Catholic Social Teaching since its inception. In his social encyclical *Centesimus Annus* (1991) Pope John Paul II considered that same desire when he examined the relationship of the market to the concept of the structures of sin. He returned once more to that constant preoccupation of Catholic Social Teaching, the rights of workers:

The obligation to earn one's bread by the sweat of one's brow also presumes the right to do so. A society in which this right is systematically denied, in which economic policies do not allow workers to reach satisfactory levels of employment, cannot be justified from an ethical point of view, nor can that society attain social peace.[12]

But, more interestingly still, he starts to makes distinctions between different varieties (or perhaps one could say degrees) of capitalism. Some on the right wing have hailed *Centesimus Annus* as an endorsement of the market economy. But, as is clear from the following passage, it frames a profound hesitation at the forces that a free market can unleash if not carefully regulated and indeed to some extent directed in the name of the common good:

Can it be said, after the failure of Communism, that capitalism is the victorious social system, and that capitalism should be the goal of the countries now making efforts to rebuild their economy and society? If by capitalism is meant an economic system which recognizes the fundamental and positive value of business, the market, private property and the resulting responsibility for the means of production, as well as free human creativity in the economic sector, then the answer is certainly in the affirmative though it would be perhaps more appropriate to speak of a business economy, market economy, or simply a free economy. But if by capitalism is meant a system in which freedom in the economic sector is not circumscribed within a strong juridical framework which places it at the service of human freedom in its totality, and which sees it as a particular aspect of that freedom, the core of which is ethical and religious, then the reply is certainly negative.[13]

We can begin to see here how very uncomfortable Pope John Paul II makes certain right-wingers feel. He is depriving them of their favourite doctrine, that is to say the doctrine of independence of political and economic action from moral and religious scrutiny. Others, reading the signs of the times – from the disintegration of the social fabric under Thatcherism to the disastrous consequences of deregulation manifest most dramatically in the arrival of 'mad cow disease' and its spread to human beings – have reached similar uneasy conclusions more instinctively. It was a theme taken up by the bishops of England and Wales in their 1996 document, *The Common Good*:

Unlimited free-market, or laissez-faire, capitalism, insists that the distribution of wealth must occur entirely according to the dictates of market forces. The theory presupposes that the good of society will take care of itself, being identified with the summation of vast numbers of individual consumer decisions in a fully competitive, and entirely free, market economy. Its central dogma (as expressed by Adam Smith, in *The Wealth of Nations*) is the belief that in an entirely free economy, each citizen, through seeking his own gain, would be 'led by an invisible hand to promote an end which was not part of his intention', namely the prosperity of society. The Catholic Church, in its social teaching, explicitly rejects belief in the automatic beneficence of market forces. It insists that the end result of market forces must be scrutinized and if necessary corrected in the name of natural law, social justice, human rights, and the common good. Left to themselves, market forces are just as likely to lead to evil results as to good ones.[14]

Faith in the beneficial consequences of market forces leaves little room for morality. And there are theorists on the right who actually reject the very concept of social justice, saying it is no more reasonable to describe a consequence of a market force as unjust than to describe the consequence of a natural force as unjust, say an earthquake or hurricane. This is where the application of the idea of 'structures of sin' to free market economic models leads us back again to the idea of solidarity and the option for the poor. For it is the poor who are most likely to suffer from over-reliance on competition to the detriment of the common good. Those who do not have wealth to spend can be gravely disadvantaged. They may also be excluded from the political processes set up to regulate the market in the name of the common good. We see this in the way that so many of the poor removed themselves from the UK electoral register in the late 1980s in an attempt to avoid paying the poll tax; even years after that regressive and unpopular tax was repealed many remain off the voting register, effectively disenfranchised within the British democratic process. It is not far-fetched, then, to conclude that free markets tend to produce what is in effect an 'option against the poor'. This concept of an 'option against the poor', was one of the truly original features of the Catholic bishops' statement and it will be interesting to note if it is ever taken up and repeated in a papal encyclical some time in the future. Capitalism necessarily contains a bias to the rich, indeed that is very nearly what the word itself means.[15] We can see here the beginnings of an objective analysis with which to contradict the so-called trickle down theory of wealth – which says that if you make the wealthy wealthier, eventually the poor will be wealthier too. A system which contains an inherent bias against the poor cannot do that. And now we can see why it cannot.

This working through of the concept of 'structures of sin' leads naturally on to the concept of liberation, and provides us a context in which we can re-examine more fruitfully the traditional clash between politics and religion. It is here that the theology of liberation can most clearly be seen as an outgrowth from Catholic Social Teaching rather than as a contradiction of it, as some of its critics have claimed. If salvation at the personal level is about our being freed from personal sin, then liberation at the social level is about our being freed from social sin. We cannot make a clear distinction between the two processes.[16] It becomes much easier to see how the church can speak of political liberation as an aspect of Christian evangelization, even to say that evangelization can never be complete while structures of sin remain to be corrected and hence while injustices exist in society. What liberation theology adds – an insight that orthodox Catholic Social Teaching has by no means rejected – is the importance of individuals being the agents of their own liberation, rather than having liberation passively done to them as if they were merely its recipients. Hence conscientization, or consciousness raising.

Since the collapse of communism in Eastern Europe and the Soviet Union in 1989, and to some extent since the abandonment of state socialism by Western European left-wing parties before and since the events of that year, capitalism itself has started to act as if it is now the only contender left on the field of battle, and therefore free to do exactly as it wills. Communism collapsed for other reasons than the obvious superiority of capitalism. It was the victim of its own internal contradictions rather than the loser in a competition to persuade the world which was the more alluring system. Capitalism has its own internal contradictions too, for capitalism is far more than just a free market – it is a system based on the artificial creation of limited liability companies, which have their own moral deficit with regard to what they take from, and give to, society. Indeed, with recession rampant in so many capitalist economies, it seemed possible in the early 1990s that the collapse of communism before the collapse of capitalism, rather than after it, was just an accident of history. Nevertheless capitalism has claimed a victory, though it also should be recorded that in *Centesimus Annus* and elsewhere, Pope John Paul II has claimed the collapse of communism as a triumph not for capitalism but for Catholic Social Teaching. And this is true, at least to the extent that the Polish trade union movement *Solidarność* was not working for the triumph of capitalism but for the recognition of basic rights, for workers and for property, that Marxism denied and the church upheld.

Capitalism's claims are likely to expand indefinitely, and as well as being an economic method capitalism will inevitably expand further into being a world-view or ideology, even a religion. Indeed there are economists on the far right for whom it is virtually a religion already; for the neo-Conservative Catholic writer Michael Novak free market economics is synonymous with the American way of life (as that is understood by right-wing libertarian Republicans). Catholic Social Teaching cannot agree. It says free markets can never be allowed to be sovereign, but must be watched, regulated and controlled, in the name of the common good. It says they are tainted by the structures of sin. It says they are biased against the poor. It says they can do harm as much as they can do good. Because people tend to need more encouragement to be unselfish than to be selfish, a moral corrective is needed to insist that a wealthy society, if it is a greedy society, is not a good society. The English bishops recognize this when they state:

The ascendancy of market-based economic models over collective or command economic models has increased the importance of Catholic Social Teaching in the modern day, especially because its own critical analysis of free-market capitalism has in no way been discredited. The Catholic Church has a long history of resistance to Marxist Communism, both as an ideology and as a power structure. But it recognizes that the very existence of this ideological opposition to capitalism, however flawed, tended in the past to act as a balancing factor or crude brake on some of the excesses of which capitalism is capable. In the light of such considerations as these, it is more necessary than ever to explain, promote and apply the Church's social teaching in the communities for which we share responsibility.[17]

In his latest social encyclical, *Centesimus Annus*, written in 1991 to mark the hundredth anniversary of *Rerum Novarum*, Pope John Paul II warns us of the future in the following terms:

In its desire to have and to enjoy rather than to be and to grow, humanity consumes the resources of the earth and its own life in an excessive and disordered way. At the root of the senseless destruction of the natural environment lies an anthropological error, which unfortunately is widespread in our day. Humanity, which discovers its capacity to transform and in a certain sense create the world through its work, forgets that this is always based on God's prior and original gift of the things that are. The human race thinks that it can make arbitrarily use of the earth, subjecting it without restraint to its will, as though the earth did not have its own requisites and a prior God-given purpose, which human beings can indeed develop but must not betray. Instead of carrying out its role as a co-operator with God in the work of creation, humanity sets itself up in place of God and thus ends up provoking a rebellion on the part of nature, which is tyrannised rather than governed.[18]

It is a gloomy vision. But Catholic Social Teaching offers an alternative. It is that idea of the common good. These two little words have stretched a long way, embracing the whole of human society and all its endeavours. They contain the implicit ideas of solidarity and subsidiarity; of the option for the poor; of public authorities answered for their care of the common good by democratic process; of the common good itself as the sum total of human rights, defended and protected by all of us for the sake of all of us; of the superiority of the human over the material and therefore the superiority of the rights of workers over the rights of capital; of the limitations of free markets and their potential to be part of the structures of sin that afflict us all; and of the environment as part of the universal common good which we must all work tirelessly to protect. These are powerful ideas, and although they collectively make up what we call Catholic Social Teaching, you don't have to be Catholic to appreciate them. They were derived from our common biblical Christian inheritance, but at a time when only the Catholic Church had enough freedom from what might be termed the downside of the Protestant ethic, including the frightening conclusion that if you were poor it was always in some way your own fault or a judgment of God for sin. The quicker these firm Christian ideas become part of the common language of all Christians engaged in politics, and indeed on the right and in the middle as well as on the left, the better it will be for the whole moral health of society and the social cohesion of its citizens.

6

The Gospel of Life: John Paul II on Spiritual Malaise and its Social Aftermath

Julie Clague

In 1995 John Paul II made perhaps his most important contribution to Catholic Social Teaching, determining the course on which future church discussions of social and political ethics will be conducted in the new millennium. The publication, in that year, of *Evangelium Vitae* – the Gospel of Life – is the culmination of his writings on social and political themes which began in 1979 with the encyclical *Redemptor Hominis*. The stated aim of *Evangelium Vitae* is to treat 'the value and inviolability of human life' but the project is in fact much broader. The theme – that we must 'respect life' – centres on familiar issues of sexual and medical ethics, but the focus on crimes against life also serves as an illustration of the morally flawed nature of the Western lifestyle and, by implication, the politico-economic model of democratic capitalism which supports it. More than his previous writings, *Evangelium Vitae* throws down the gauntlet to challenge the value system of Western society.

The originality and significance of *Evangelium Vitae* lies in its attempt to draw together politics, economics and morality into one coherent picture by combining the familiar subject matter of Catholic Social Teaching with church teachings on medical and sexual ethics. The result is an ambitious synthesis and amplification of themes central to the corpus of John Paul's writings. The 1991 encyclical *Centesimus Annus* – concerned with socialism, capitalism, democracy and Godlessness – is the most obvious prequel to *Evangelium Vitae*. It outlines many themes, including the idea that the Western world is in the grip of a 'culture of death', which are further elaborated in *Evangelium Vitae*. It also relies on the treatment of fundamental morals in *Veritatis Splendour* (1993) and the theory of structural sin, formulated in *Sollicitudo Rei Socialis* (1987). It re-iterates teachings on which John Paul has been vocal, from those outlined before his papacy such as the Congregation for the Doctrine of the Faith's *Declaration on Procured Abortion* (1974) to its pronouncements under him on Euthanasia (1980) and *Donum Vitae* (On Respect for Human Life) (1987). There is, therefore, little which is remarkable by way of discontinuity with previous teaching, or new in terms of subject matter (the treatment of the death penalty being the obvious exception – he expresses far more serious reservations about the occasions on which it might be justified than the Vatican has ever done previously). However, to the extent that *Evangelium Vitae* is a work of integration, it is perhaps the most significant encyclical which Pope John Paul has written.

The strategy employed in *Evangelium Vitae* stems from the assumption that personal assessments of issues in medical and sexual ethics are not 'private morality', as they are often mistakenly described, but very public – both in the effects they have on society and because they are born from cultural attitudes which are dependent on a politico-economic climate which is conducive to their flourishing. Thus, contraception and abortion are described as 'fruits of the same tree' in that they can both be products of a hedonistic mentality 'which regards procreation as an obstacle to personal fulfilment'.[1] Hedonism, widespread in the West, thrives when it has the necessary conditions of individual liberty and relative affluence which democratic capitalism provides.

While Roman Catholics are expected to regard all papal teaching as authoritative, in practice Catholic Social Teaching has been little publicized by comparison with the church's moral teaching on sexual and medical ethics. Such differentiation between so-called 'social' and 'personal' morality was generally facilitated by their separate treatment in papal pronouncements. In *Evangelium Vitae* the two are intertwined, making any distinction between them less clear whilst also suggesting their mutual reinforcement; combined they create a powerful impression of the West's moral malaise. The importance of this strategy should be underlined. *Evangelium Vitae* provides the most comprehensive picture and unequivocal statement of John Paul's world view and makes the subsequent room for manoeuvre of his successor all the more limited by binding the church's doctrine on social issues to its teaching on personal morality.

Secularism and moral disintegration

On the cusp of the new millennium the global agenda is still in the process of being reshaped following the collapse of the iron curtain. The demise of totalitarian communism and the portrayal of the capitalist West as victor has required a papal response. Karol Wojtyla, with his Polish background, has been supremely placed as an authoritative commentator on the historic events of the late twentieth century. But John Paul also sees himself as an actor on the world stage: his role as leader of the Roman Catholic Church has allowed him to influence history. He was chosen to be pope at a moment when history most needed him – that is clearly John Paul's own self-understanding: providence guides him. He believes the Polish Catholic Church, of which he is a part, had a role to play in bringing communism to an end.

The Cold War is over, but the battle between good and evil is not yet won. 'On the eve of the Third Millennium, the challenge facing us is an arduous one: only the concerted efforts of all those who believe in the value of life can prevent a setback of unforeseeable consequences for civilization.'[2] Humankind, despite the march of 'progress', is still faced with an apparent inability to deliver peace and justice to the majority of people in the world. Rather than tackling such pressing problems, those in a position to address them appear bent on moral disintegration. And the economic mechanism which assisted the defeat of communism is now more adversary than ally. So, although the millennium should symbolize the dawning of a new era, the struggle is not yet over. Such is the context in which *Evangelium Vitae* is written. There is a looming sense of crisis. Loyalty, strength, courage, heroism and perhaps martyrdom will be required in this moral campaign. *Evangelium Vitae* accepts the sometimes tragic ambiguity which characterizes complex societies, whereby our actions and decisions inevitably have both good and bad effects. This is seen, for example, in the discussion of abortion.[3] However, the pope does not want to make too many concessions to ambiguity. John Paul inhabits a moral universe which has no black holes or gaps. All questions can be answered; there is no place for doubt. Strong rules make for clear teaching; weak rules lead to moral uncertainty.

As many commentators have noted, John Paul's theological outlook is broadly Augustinian, and this influence is clear throughout the encyclical. Echoing Augustine's *City of God*, the structure of *Evangelium Vitae* is built around the rhetorical device of two opposing world views: the culture of life and the culture of death. These contrasting cultures are presented in John Paul's idiosyncratic style – a style which has evident parallels with that of Augustine. Augustine's mode of communication has been captured vividly by John Mahoney:

> It may be suggested, in fact, that for much of the time Augustine does not make distinctions, he offers dramatic alternatives, highly charged opposing poles. He is not a logician or a Schoolman, but a most skilful rhetorician who is disposed more to set up extremes than to explore the middle ground between them . . . So often with Augustine it appears to be all or nothing, black or white, which he has to offer . . .[4]

Evangelium Vitae combines piety with rhetoric, exhortation with argument. The message is continually repeated. Scripture is invoked in homiletic style. The language used is often extreme, urgent and powerful. According to Gary Lysaght: 'The Pope writes like van Gogh paints: broad strokes, huge amounts of paint, strong colours. For the subtle nuances, for almost mathematical precision, we need to look elsewhere, to the theological equivalent of a Vermeer, perhaps.'[5]

John Paul's critique of communism was based largely on its anti-religious aspect. However, the prosperous West has also edged God to the margins through technological and economic progress. The pope identifies this as one of the causes of the West's moral decay, for denial of God involves denial of God's plan for humanity. 'Where God is denied and people live as though he did not exist, or his commandments are not taken into account, the dignity of the human person and the inviolability of human life also end up being rejected or compromised,'[6] he writes. Life is devalued when it is no longer seen as a sacred gift of God.[7] Materialism results whereby 'the values of *being* are replaced by those of *having*'.[8] Humankind in its weakness worships false gods in the hope that they will provide the happiness that only the true God can provide. The idols we worship may be mammon, pleasure, technology, freedom from commitments or the deification of efficiency. It is an idolatry of which Christians and non-Christians alike are guilty.

The pope's reflections on the contemporary denial of God and God's truth are reminiscent of Augustine's concerns in the *City Of God*, a central tenet of which is that true virtue can only exist where there is true worship of the true God.[9] Augustine argues against the worship of false gods and the moral excesses which such worship provokes. For John Paul, as for Augustine, the idea of morality without God is in some way deficient. In seeking to address the complacency of Western Christians John Paul maintains, firstly, that Christians should not separate their faith from social responsibility. Secondly, Christians are a part of the world, but too many have become conformed to the world's priorities and lost sight of the values of the kingdom. Even Christians are making moral decisions which are contrary to the gospel.[10]

William Temple once wrote: 'The method of the Church's impact upon society at large should be twofold. The Church must announce Christian principles and point out where the existing social order at any time is in conflict with them. It must then pass on to Christian citizens, acting in their civic capacity, the task of re-shaping the existing order in closer conformity to the principles.'[11] This, effectively, is the task of Catholic Social Teaching in general and usefully summarizes the aim of *Evangelium Vitae*. In so far as the gospel of life is obscured by modern living, the church is charged with the mission of evangelization.

According to *Evangelium Vitae*, within the culture of death the weak are increasingly under threat from the powerful. Despite eloquent articulations of human rights, an excessive rightism has emerged alongside an ironic disregard for human rights in practice – particularly the right to life. Crucially, crimes against life such as the practice of abortion and euthanasia are gaining acceptance, even within the supposedly life-promoting unit of the family. The root of this crisis is, the pope claims, because old certainties about human nature, the moral order and humankind's relationship to God have been replaced by uncertainty and scepticism. The culture of death is not an isolated or chance occurrence, but is 'actively fostered by powerful cultural, economic and political currents which encourage an idea of society excessively concerned with efficiency'.[12] In such an economic and cultural climate, families are prone to fragmentation both across generations and geographically, and their decisive work at the service of life is made more difficult. The potential consequences for society are disastrous, for the family plays an essential role in establishing the culture of life. Therefore support must be given to families: 'A family policy must be the basis and driving force of all social policies.'[13]

Despite the pessimistic tone of the discussion, *Evangelium Vitae* recognizes that positive signs of an alternative culture are discernible through various initiatives of support for the weak: families who accept abandoned children; those who help mothers in difficulty; medical developments for the sick and dying; international aid and so on. He notes a new sensitivity in favour of ecology and against war; increased commitment to non-violence and a growing opposition to the death penalty. Many campaign against abortion and euthanasia. In all these areas, the church is visible in providing charitable help. These are signs of the gospel of life which, in contrast to the culture of death, derives from a belief in the inherent dignity of the person who is called to a fullness of life which transcends the bounds of earthly existence to include a sharing in the life of God. Although, in its first footnote, the encyclical concedes that 'The expression "Gospel of Life" is not found as such in Sacred Scripture', it nevertheless goes on to state: 'In effect, the absolute inviolability of innocent human life is a moral truth clearly taught by Sacred Scripture, constantly upheld in the Church's Tradition and consistently proposed by her Magisterium.' Hence, John Paul proclaims (in a type of infallible-speak): 'by the authority which Christ conferred upon Peter and his Successors, and in communion with the Bishops of the Catholic Church, *I confirm that the direct and voluntary killing of an innocent human being is always gravely immoral*.'[14] Whether one is ultimately persuaded by the content and argumentation of *Evangelium Vitae* depends to a considerable degree on one's acceptance of this moral norm as absolute. Those who doubt the validity of this formulation – which admits no exceptions – as applied to the concrete cases to which the encyclical refers (namely abortion, euthanasia and – most controversially – suicide) are likely also to question other aspects of the encyclical such as the permissible degree of involvement and co-operation of medical personnel in abortion and euthanasia. They will also question the encyclical's view that state laws which permit the taking of innocent human life are unjust and should be overturned. John Paul admits no such reservations. He is so certain of the prohibition's enduring and immutable character, that for him the requirement of a restrictive public policy becomes inevitable.

The extreme dichotomy utilized by *Evangelium Vitae* may be useful as a device for communicating a message and adding urgency to the argument, but it is not without its weaknesses. Such a dualistic approach tends to distort and simplify positions: Church versus world, gospel versus culture, good versus evil. Reality is seldom so oppositional. Dualisms can foster an 'us and them' attitude which is counter-productive. It becomes so easy for us (the good guys) to scapegoat them (the bad guys) that we embrace triumphalism and certainty while losing sight of the possible fallibility of our own position (recall the qualifying insertion of 'in effect' in the sentence about the absolute inviolability of innocent human life above). It is also a false dichotomy, in so far as virtually no one intentionally sides with the culture of death, which is a caricature of reality. The real picture is more subtle. True, the culture of death as described in *Evangelium Vitae* reflects real tendencies which are prevalent in our society and which lose sight of important values or mis-prioritize them. But even those who support abortion and euthanasia genuinely believe such activities promote other values which are important for humanity; they are not totally nihilistic. The notion of 'quality of life', for example, would be one such value – itself mentioned in *Evangelium Vitae* as 'a welcome sign'.[15] However, leaving aside the question of the stylistic merits of the encyclical, there are important aspects to John Paul's analysis which demand closer attention.

Two features in particular, which are said to characterize the culture of death, are given prominence in the encyclical: the desire to maximize freedom (individual liberty) and the desire to control (technological applications in the interests of efficiency). The former is pursued at the micro level by self-centred consumers[16] and encouraged at the macro level by a capitalist society content to legislate for liberty since collectively it is unable to agree on the correct ordering of values.[17] The latter manifests itself at the micro level in the individual's desire for control over life and death – often by utilizing ever more efficient scientific products.[18] At the macro level technological control leads to economic control; witness society's insatiable desire for increased economic efficiency.[19]

Economic efficiency, social justice or personal liberty?

According to John Maynard Keynes: 'The political problem of mankind is to combine three things: economic efficiency, social justice and individual liberty.'[20] No industrial society can function effectively without these three elements; attempts to discard them are folly. The problem is one of balance, of holding the three in a creative harmony. It is a problem which taxes the West, but which is not peculiar to it; neither is it solely a feature of capitalism nor of democracy. Rather it is characteristic of modernity as a whole. It is the subject of scrutiny for politicians, philosophers, economists and sociologists. It is *the* question and the solution is elusive. *Evangelium Vitae*, of course, is concerned with the excesses of economic efficiency and individual liberty and the negative effects these have on social justice.

On the first of these – economic efficiency – *Evangelium Vitae* says: 'The criterion of personal dignity – which demands respect, generosity and service – is replaced by the criterion of efficiency, functionality and usefulness: others are considered not for what they "are", but for what they "have, do and produce". This is the supremacy of the strong over the weak.'[21] Increasingly, technology is transforming scientific knowledge into a marketable product which can be bought and sold in the interests of productive efficiency.[22] This brings about rapid cultural transformation or what the Vatican II document, *Gaudium et Spes*, described as the 'accelerated pace of history'. However, where *Gaudium et Spes* was basically optimistic about the possibilities of 'progress', *Evangelium Vitae* is more cautious. Rather than technology being at the service of humankind, human needs are being sacrificed in the interests of economic efficiency. Man is being reduced to *homo oeconomicus*. Market forces replace moral values as the impetus for technological innovation and progress is judged in terms of economic growth. The powerful gain while the weak lose out when efficiency is the god.

John Paul's criticisms of efficiency and certain applications of technology are trenchant. In this respect John Paul resembles Jean-Jacques Rousseau (1712–78), who believed – contrary to many of his Enlightenment contemporaries – that the scientific and technological progress of the Industrial Revolution was corrupting mankind. Rousseau argued that industrialization led to materialism and exploitation. He believed the rich were unjustly dominating the poor in a sort of social contract. Wealth was a false pleasure which led to unfulfilment. True happiness was to be found by those closest to nature. One would not want to press the similarity between the two men too far, but Rousseau's reservations about the Industrial Revolution find parallels in *Evangelium Vitae*'s concern over the effects of the technological revolution. The thirsty capitalist engine must still be sated.

The second area where John Paul II feels the Keynesian political equation is out of balance is in an excessive modern emphasis on individual liberty. He says: ' . . . God gives everyone freedom, a freedom which possesses an *inherently relational dimension* . . . but when freedom is made absolute in an individualistic way, it is emptied of its original content, and its very meaning and dignity are contradicted.'[23] *Evangelium Vitae* rejects the extreme view of individual liberty which says 'you do your thing and I'll do mine'. To say that constitutes a radical individualism which denies our connectedness, that is, the social dimension of existence. A vicious circle swiftly results: as distorted notions of freedom lead to further fragmentation of society so, in turn, the divided society breeds more autonomous individuals. Such autonomy leads to a suspicion and rejection of others who are seen as enemies: 'Other people are not rivals from whom we must defend ourselves, but brothers and sisters to be supported.'[24]

Many fear that social cohesion, if it ever existed, has dissolved to leave, at best, simple co-existence and toleration of difference. Indeed, some question whether social cohesion is possible today. According to this view, since we inhabit increasingly pluralist societies, in which there exist differing conceptions of the good, there is no common morality which we can share. This is considered a depressing scenario to many, for history teaches us that in such circumstances, might becomes right. Hegemony is the direct consequence of ethical relativism. The liberal philosopher Richard Rorty has argued: ' . . . if we take care of political and cultural freedom, truth and rationality will take care of themselves'.[25] According to *Evangelium Vitae*, this is just not true. John Paul would argue that individual liberty must restrict itself in the interests of moral truth: when freedom shuts out the truth about good and evil all that remains is opinion and choice.[26] Augustine's key insight that evil in the world arises as a direct consequence of humankind's misuse of freedom is given contemporary articulation in *Evangelium Vitae*. God created humans with the freedom to choose good over evil; but just as creation is ongoing, so is the fall: humans have disordered goals and consequently make disordered choices.

Evangelium Vitae therefore rejects as unhealthy the desire for absolute freedom and complete control over our lives which is very much the spirit of the age. Western societies tend to promote both of these to the detriment of other important human values. Brian Griffiths, once head of Margaret Thatcher's Policy Unit, has argued that the tension between the desire to be free and the desire for control is the root of the crisis then afflicting East and West. Humanism, he suggests, has been unable to satisfy the desire for freedom and the desire for control:

> Because Marxism like humanism is also the product of an Enlightenment view of the world, the practical problems of both capitalism and communism are seen to have a common origin – namely the inability of humanism as a philosophy to resolve the basic tension between freedom and control. Capitalism suffers from inflation, instability, pollution and injustice because of inadequate limits on the exercise of freedom. Communism suffers from the direction of capital and labour and state control of the family, religion, education and the arts, because of inadequate limits on the urge to dominate . . . From a Christian point of view therefore the root cause of the crisis of capitalism is not bigger government or more complex technology or even defects in the system of property rights, but certain false values on which it is based.[27]

Griffith's analysis applies to political systems but his general argument is heading in the same direction as that of *Evangelium Vitae*.

In a sense freedom and control are curious bedfellows, since they tend to be oppositional. Human freedom undermines control and control seeks to circumscribe freedom. However, both are given simultaneous expression in one crucial area of activity: we exercise our freedom and assert our control through the choices we make. People have always made choices, but the modern world presents us with an unprecedented array of decisions. Today, we demand choice in the supermarkets, we demand choice over education, health provision, and so on. The increase in choices available to people is a peculiarly modern phenomenon. This contrasts with the mediaeval world where choices were limited: individuals did not have the power to choose for themselves what to believe, how to live or who should govern them.

In the medical and sexual sphere, increased choice largely stems from the greater number of interventions now possible in nature, where otherwise there would be chance not choice. The moral task is to determine which choices are humanizing, according to which values are promoted or denied by the decision. The pro–choice position tends to absolutize choice itself, rather than the features which make the choice good or bad, that is, the values at stake in the decision. The dominant mode of address for individuals in the West has become that of consumer, not citizen. Market forces are simply the measure of consumers making choices. In a consumer society there is incredulity that there may exist some things to which no one has a right. We live in a world where money buys most things and we are accustomed to an attitude which says 'I want it, I can pay for it so let me have it.' Rightsism emerges in which individuals and groups claim for themselves – using the language of rights as a currency of social negotiation – a greater degree of freedom to control their destiny than can be sustained without impinging on the rights of other individuals and groups.

But we see a profound irony in our moral choices and decision-making today. It is at its most ironic in the modern hospital. Within the same specialism there are those choosing to have babies through the utilization of reproductive technology and those choosing to terminate pregnancies. There are those struggling to live, and others wishing to die, both groups seeking the assistance of medical personnel. It illustrates the value-dissonance which free choice creates.

The problem of democracy

All of this ethical and economic interplay takes place within a political context. The science of choice when applied to the political community is known as democracy. During the twentieth century Catholicism has moved away from approving authoritarian modes of government (at least, outside of the way the church governs itself). Its stated preference is for the participatory model which democracy provides. Whereas, at the turn of the century, Pope Leo XIII refrained from indicating a preferred political model,[28] 1960s Catholic Social Teaching made explicit mention of the value of democracy.[29] However, democracy is something with which John Paul is not altogether comfortable and he has not been uncritical of its philosophical underpinnings.[30] John Paul's assessment of democracy can only be understood as part of a unified theory in which godlessness, moral relativism, individualism and the rule of the majority are causally related and interdependent. The state should be bound by duty to God, and laws framed according to truth and justice. But in democracies, authorities are subject not to the law of God but to the will of the people. Once there is a rejection of divine authority to whom obedience is due, man becomes a law to himself. Having lost the sense of and need for a transcendent Other guiding humanity, the case for any locus of moral truth (and source of duty) fades. In both sentiment and argumentation, John Paul's writing is reminiscent of his predecessor Leo XIII (not least in its Augustinian leanings). Indeed, the concerns John Paul expresses in *Evangelium Vitae* and its precursor *Centesimus Annus* find corresponding parallels in Leo's encyclical *On The Christian Constitution Of States*.[31]

In short, John Paul's attitude to democracy is ambivalent; democracy is more valuable for what it prevents (totalitarianism) than what it creates. It is better than the alternatives, but not ideal in itself. Any student of democracy knows that, in practice, it has many inherent weaknesses, but some still smugly maintain that democracy has right automatically on its side. It is a view which the encyclical is at pains to repudiate:

> If today we see an almost universal consensus with regard to the value of democracy, this is to be considered a positive 'sign of the times', as the Church's Magisterium has frequently noted. But the value of democracy stands or falls with the values which it embodies and promotes.[32]

In other words, democracy and morality are not synonymous. The pope's discussion of democracy takes place in the context of civil laws which permit abortion and euthanasia. *Evangelium Vitae* insists that civil law should be in accordance with the moral law. Laws which seek to legitimate abortion and euthanasia are 'intrinsically unjust': 'There is no obligation in conscience to obey such laws; instead there is a *grave and clear obligation to oppose them by conscientious objection.*'[33] The encyclical condemns liberal laws which give citizens the freedom to choose abortion and euthanasia, instead favouring restrictive legislation in which freedom is limited in the interests of the common good. However, it is difficult to see how such legislation could ever be feasible (due to problems of compliance) in societies where many citizens do not share the church's absolutist moral stance. *Evangelium Vitae* therefore advises Christians to use the mechanisms of democracy to defend life and, where there are strong opposing outlooks, to achieve the best possible compromise.

An alternative position, which *Evangelium Vitae* rejects,[34] states that pluralistic societies should legislate in ways which present their citizens with maximum freedom of choice. Lawmakers should respect the diversity of opinion which exists and allow citizens to balance the values themselves rather than impose values in paternalistic fashion; it is not the task of the law to choose between different moral outlooks nor to impose one view on others. This appears to be the position of the Catholic theologian Michael Novak, at least in his book *The Spirit of Democratic*

Capitalism. When speaking of the failure of communism he stated: 'The enforcement of high ideals by coercion of law has been tried before'.[35] He argues that Christianity cannot be imposed on democratic capitalism:

> Individual Christians and their organized bodies may legitimately work through democratic means to shape the will of the majority; but they must also observe the rights of others and, more than that, heed practical wisdom by respecting the consciences of others even more than the law might demand. On the question of abortion, for example, no one is ever likely to be satisfied with the law, but all might be well advised not to demand in law all that their own conscience demands . . . In the world at large, moreover, the consciences of all Christians are not identical. An economy based on the consciences of some would offend the consciences of others.[36]

This is one area where more work is required. The second position has an obvious attraction for policy makers working in pluralist societies. Permissive laws promote personal autonomy. No one is compelled to act contrary to their consciences (at least, not theoretically). However, laws geared towards individual freedom can fail to take account of potentially damaging social effects. In the case of euthanasia legislation, for example, such negative effects could include compromising the role of the medical profession; undermining trust in the doctor-patient relationship; devaluing society's attitude towards life; increased pressure on the elderly to request euthanasia out of an unwillingness to be a burden on others; and from the possibility that the law would be open to abuse and impossible to police.

The problem of how to legislate when there is a division of opinion on moral matters illustrates the crisis for liberal democracies. How should the state arbitrate when citizens disagree on the content of the common good? According to John Paul: 'It is impossible to further the common good without acknowledging and defending the right to life, upon which all the other inalienable rights of individuals are founded and from which they develop.'[37] However, despite the eloquent simplicity of the pope's message, the fact still remains that there is not unanimous agreement about the moral wrongness of abortion and euthanasia. Sometimes, in a democracy, freedom to do wrong is valued more highly than enforcing good behaviour.

Majoritarianism, in which majority decision determines public policy, is frequently seen as the solution to moral disagreement. However, for John Paul – as for Leo XIII before him[38] – majoritarianism is a major weakness of democracy, and one which threatens the common good. Decisions about the right to life become 'subject to the will of the stronger part.'[39] How should one respond when the majority favours something which offends one's conscience? John Paul's frustration lies in the fact that the current Western system gives people the political freedom and economic means to make choices (which totalitarianism denied) but is unable to direct their choices towards moral truth.

The pope's strategy, therefore, is to recommend the prohibition of some immoral choices (abortion and euthanasia) thereby placing them 'out of the game', beyond the scope of the democratic process. One wonders whether this is one instance in which John Paul would find the political model of authoritarianism preferable to democracy. If democracy is the political manifestation of the value of freedom and authoritarianism is the political manifestation of the value of control, the pope would instinctively choose the latter rather than the former as the surest means to the common good. One need only look to the current internal ordering of the institutional Catholic Church for confirmation of this. John Paul is evidently uneasy with democratic systems in which there is no paternalistic 'trump card' to guarantee 'right' decisions. Liberalism, which emphasizes personal freedom, finds this position untenable. When given a choice between paternalism (an authority figure defining what is in others' best interests) and autonomy (individuals determining their own best interests), liberalism always chooses autonomy. Liberalism remains agnostic about moral truth and the common good therefore becomes, at most, a set of instrumental conditions for harmonious communal living based on the maximization of individual freedom. For a church which believes that moral truth has been revealed, the content of the common good becomes definable and paternalism a live option as a means to its delivery.

Yet if both systems are capable of delivering the common good, why has Catholicism in its general pronouncements eschewed paternalism in favour of participatory government? The short answer is that democracy is subsidiarity in action: social decisions are taken at the lowest possible level. John Paul is right to remain cautious about what democracy can deliver. Yet one suspects that his preferred strategy for dealing with the difficult problems which democracy poses involves the sort of paternalistic interventions which Catholicism has sought to reject in other spheres. Clearly, the church would benefit from further reflection on the issues which *Evangelium Vitae* raises concerning the morally problematic aspects of democracy.

Ambitious though it is, and definitive though John Paul II may have hoped to make it, *Evangelium Vitae* does not offer a comprehensively satisfactory position on all the issues which the pope set out to address. What is clear, however, is the extent to which John Paul's writing is in continuity with the tradition of Catholic Social Teaching, but how it also carries it forward through the introduction of new themes and fresh emphases. In keeping with pre-Wojtyla social teaching, John Paul's writings start from a vision of the inviolable dignity of the human person and its expression in an articulation of human rights. The basic conviction is that social existence is the way in which humans best flourish. There is a concern for the family as the basic social unit, a commitment to the weak and oppressed and calls for the removal of unjust structures which deny basic human rights.

Catholic Social Teaching is not radical, in the sense of extreme; quite the opposite. It is safe and moderate. The task is always one of balance, promoting human well-being by avoiding the extremes of individualism and collectivism. It wants human rights but rejects rightsism; it wants peace but knows pacifism is not always pragmatic; it calls for reform of society but not revolution; it points out flaws in existing social models but resists proposing alternatives; it asserts the equality of men and women but also their complementarity. Catholic Social Teaching argues for the transformation of society, but avoids upsetting the status quo. There is a presumption in favour of the current systems and a desire for them to work effectively – for example, for world poverty to be alleviated by a more just capitalism. It remains agnostic about the sort of politico-economic model which is required to deliver human well-being. Instead it is up to the real lives of individuals to seek to eradicate poverty, injustice and so on. That is, Christians working within the existing order and using the mechanisms that order provides.

What makes Catholic Social Teaching remarkable is that, with its goal firmly set on the establishment of God's kingdom, it is future-oriented. It believes there is a better world than the present, but unlike ideological systems it is not so arrogant as to propose how that world can come about. Humanity is constantly called to transcend itself, but the mystery of that process is the work of grace. Catholic Social Teaching, therefore, is forward-looking and carries a moral imperative. Contrast this with those who, through scepticism and complacency, have lost the ability to envisage futures which are better. The best of Catholic Social Teaching is, above all, hopeful and it is this which gives its message a momentum as we perch on the end of an era and look to the new millennium.

7

Into the Twenty-First Century: John Paul II and the New Millennium

Paul Vallely

The new millennium brings with it a new political landscape. Economically, the financial and industrial activities of the world are becoming one. Ideologically, the domination of the free market, since the fall of communism, goes universally unchallenged. Yet socially there is a growing sense of fragmentation and rootlessness with which most societies seem ill at ease. The ground seems ripe to receive the insights which Catholic Social Teaching has developed over a century of analysis and thought.

Pope John Paul II has prepared for the new age with an encyclical in 1994 called *Tertio Millennio Adveniente* (Towards the Third Millennium) which offers some pointers on the application of these to the twenty-first century. The pope begins on a big canvas. There are no mysterious millennial or cosmic cycles in history, he says, but there is a sense of the importance of time for Christians who have a duty to sanctify it, to mark it, to use it well:

> The whole of Christian history appears to us as a single river, into which many tributaries pour their waters. The year 2000 invites us to gather with renewed fidelity and ever deeper communion along the banks of this great river: the river of revelation, of Christianity and of the church, a river which flows through human history starting from the event which took place at Nazareth and then at Bethlehem 2,000 years ago.[1]

From there he insists that the first task incumbent on the church in preparing for the next 1,000 years is an examination of its collective conscience and an apology for its wrong-doing in the past. It must enter the new millennium with a clear awareness of what has happened to it during the last ten centuries – recalling all those times in history when its members departed from the spirit of Christ and his Gospel – and encouraging them to 'purify themselves, through repentance, of past errors and instances of infidelity, inconsistency and slowness to act'.[2] In particular it must repent of its past intolerance and use of violence. 'Acknowledging the weaknesses of the past is an act of honesty and courage which helps us to strengthen our faith, which alerts us to face today's temptations and challenges, and prepares us to meet them.'[3] He is not specific but it is not hard to make a list of such faults, from the church's historic connivance in sexism and anti-semitism, through the Inquisition and its acquiescence of slavery, to its early opposition to democracy and more recently the involvement of many Christians in the violation of fundamental human rights by totalitarian regimes.

'The best preparation for the new millennium,' the encyclical says, 'can only be expressed in a renewed commitment to apply, as faithfully as possible, the teachings of Vatican II to the life of every individual and of the whole church.'[4] It is a time for 'an increased sensitivity to all that the Spirit is saying to the church and to the churches, as well as to individuals through charisms meant to serve the whole community. The purpose is to emphasize what the Spirit is suggesting to the different communities, from the smallest ones, such as the family, to the largest ones, such as nations and international organizations, taking into account cultures, societies and sound traditions.'[5] In the church this will mean 'a greater attention to the voice of the Spirit through the acceptance of charisms and the promotion of the laity, a deeper commitment to the cause of Christian unity and the increased interest in dialogue with other religions and with contemporary culture'.[6] There is even a suggestion that this might extend to the insights of other faiths.[7]

The urgency of Third World Debt relief

Yet always there are reservations. 'However,' warns the pope, casting his eyes towards the problems of dialogue with the religions of the East, 'care will always have be taken not to cause harmful misunderstandings, avoiding the risk of syncretism and of a facile and deceptive irenicism.'[8] As if in confirmation, not long after publication of *Tertio Millennio Adveniente*, John Paul II sanctioned the excommunication (since revoked) of one of Asia's leading liberation theologians, Tissa Balasuriya, a priest from Sri Lanka who had been engaged in dialogue with Hindus and Buddhists; it was a move against dissent which went a step further than the pope had felt necessary in the decade before when the Swiss theologian Hans Küng, the American Charles Curran and several others were declared to be no longer 'Catholic' theologians and the Vatican demanded a vow of silence from the Brazilian liberation theologian Leonardo Boff.

The caveats in *Tertio Millennio Adveniente* extend even to the Second Vatican Council which transformed the church in the 1960s. An end-of-millennium examination of conscience must also consider the reception given by the church to Vatican II. John Paul calls the revolutionary council 'this great gift of the Spirit to the church at the end of the second millennium'.[9] Yet has it, he asks, really strengthened the church? Do present-day attitudes to it 'leave room for charisms, ministries and different forms of participation by the people of God, without adopting notions borrowed from democracy and sociology which do not reflect the Catholic vision of the church and the authentic spirit of Vatican II?'[10]

His reservations are those he has aired elsewhere before. The Pope restates his anxieties about the insidious creep of secularism. He talks of religious indifference among Christians, of a loss of their sense of the transcendent in human life, of ethical relativism, moral uncertainty and theological confusion. Few would doubt that in doing so the pope once again pinpoints some of the areas in which the modern world has lost sight of important values or skewed their priorities. But his black and white world view allows

no room for dialogue with those who want to weave consequential-
ist insights into the framework of absolute values; rather, the
solutions he offers are stark. He calls on Christians to turn with
renewed interest to the sacraments, to promote the family and
marriage, and to demand a call to return to fidelity of the martyrs
– on whom there are extensive passages. Above all he calls
Catholics to 'a more mature awareness of their own responsibilities, as well as to a more lively sense of the importance of ecclesial
obedience'.[11] The echoes of *Veritatis Splendor* are unmistakable,
with its insistence that 'opposition to the teaching of the Church's
pastors cannot be seen as legitimate expressions either of Christian
Freedom or of the diversity of the Spirit's gifts'.[12]

As the new millennium dawns Pope John Paul's eyes are not
upon the wider world. They are turned inwards, to the church
itself. It might be argued that social issues ought not to be, in this
encyclical, his chief focus; he is, after all, first concerned with the
two thousandth anniversary of the birth of his church's founder.
But he does also ask Christians to turn their gaze outwards to consider what Pope John XXIII called 'the signs of the times' – those
manifestations of God's continuing creation which can be detected
outside the church:

> There is also a need for a better appreciation and understanding
> of the signs of hope present in the last part of this century, even
> though they often remain hidden from our eyes. In society in
> general, such signs of hope include: scientific, technological and
> especially medical progress in the service of human life, a greater
> awareness of our responsibility for the environment, efforts to
> restore peace and justice wherever they have been violated, a
> desire for reconciliation and solidarity among different peoples,
> particularly in the complex relationship between the North and
> the South of the world.[13]

In this he expresses particular concerns on the question of
Third World Debt. The new millennium, says *Tertio Millennio
Adveniente*, must begin with a greater emphasis on the church's

preferential option for the poor and the outcast. The year 2000 is to be a Year of Jubilee. In ancient Israel every seventh year, according to the law of Moses, was the 'sabbatical year' during which the earth was left fallow and slaves were set free; in addition the law also provided for the cancellation of all debts in accordance with precise regulations. The Old Testament logic was that those who possessed these goods as personal property were really only stewards; God remains the sole owner and it is God's will that created goods should serve everyone in a just way. Thus every fifty years was a 'jubilee' year in which these mechanisms for restoring the equilibrium of society were most comprehensively required. To press for their modern equivalent at the year 2000, the pope says, 'Christians will have to raise their voice on behalf of all the poor of the world, proposing the jubilee as an appropriate time to give thought, among other things, to reducing substantially, if not cancelling outright, the international debt which seriously threatens the future of many nations.'[14] Work on this specific issue has begun to gather momentum with the international Jubilee 2000 movement, mobilizing hundreds of thousands of Christians worldwide, though as yet failing to make serious impact on the leaders of the world's industrial powers.

Yet *Tertio Millennio Adveniente* is significant to Catholic Social Teaching in a wider way because it draws us again into the territory of John Paul's unease with democracy. And this is a key area in which the church's teaching has to develop in the future if it is to have serious influence upon that new political landscape which is currently being formed – a landscape of opportunity and of danger – in a plural society, which is multi-cultural and multi-faith, and where Christians have to make their contribution through persuasion rather than dogmatic statement.

Democracy and authority

It is in his fear of democracy that John Paul's social teachings bumps up against a severe internal contradiction. The pope was a strong advocate of democracy when totalitarian communism was on the scene. But its chief virtue for the Polish pope lay in the greater evil it kept out. Once communism had fallen, democracy was exposed as a majoritarian iniquity in which the will of the majority could enslave the truth. Here the political and economic ability to make choices is no guarantee of moral truth. The commitment to human freedom was what, he believes, allowed the West to win the Cold War. Yet the terrible irony was that the West, even as it fought that battle, was undermining that commitment to freedom by the widespread adoption of a relativist philosophy.

There is some truth in this. In the end relativism – with its insistence that all value systems are of equal status – is always self-defeating: it is what allows the Nazi to justify killing the Jew, the cannibal to eat his vanquished foes, or the misogynist to act as if women were inferior. Yet the pope seems unaware of the irony that his own authoritarian attitudes also conflict with that affirmation of freedom.

He aired his concerns over democracy again more recently in 1997 in an address to the Pontifical Academy of Social Sciences in Rome. 'Democracy is only possible', he said, 'on the basis of a correct conception of the human person which involves the recognition of the right of every person to take an active part in public life with a view to achieving the common good.'[15] How, he asked the Academicians who had gathered to discuss the relationship between democracy and work, can someone who is not properly respected at the economic level – and lacks even the basic necessities – be guaranteed participation in democratic life? That question is one where there may be scope for resolution in exploring mechanisms of democracy and also different approaches to what constitutes work, as we shall consider in the Epilogue. But it became clear that at the root of John Paul's concerns about democracy are laws passed, with majority approval, which permit abortion or euthanasia. 'When even the right to life, from conception to its natural end, is not fully respected as an absolute inalienable right, democracy is undermined and the formal rules for participation become an alibi that conceals the tyranny of the strong over the weak.'[16]

There is a contradiction at the heart of the pope's strategy here.[17] In *Evangelium Vitae* he declared that (a) abortion was always wrong and (b) any destruction of a human embryo, from the moment of conception, had to be regarded as abortion. This, he said, was an exercise of his Magisterium, in order to put the matter beyond doubt. But in so doing he implicitly admitted that invoking the Magisterium was necessary to settle what would otherwise be disputed questions. Hence abortion (at least in category (b) above) was no longer something everyone knew in their hearts was wrong. They only knew it if they were Catholics, guided by the church. For the majority of non-Catholics, the notion that an early embryo has full human rights is untenable. Rights in that sense are something a foetus accumulates as it grows, until by some point like twenty-two or twenty-four weeks, often associated with quickening, most people appear to accept that a foetus should enjoy a legal status and protection. What the pope neglects is that elsewhere in Catholic teaching, on freedom of conscience, non-Catholics cannot be assumed to be bound by the judgments of the Magisterium. That is to say his rulings (a) and (b) were binding on Catholics only – and this, according to Catholic theology itself. And by making his ruling, he was admitting that without the guidance of the Catholic Church, people would not know these truths about abortion, or at least not know them for certain. Thus a democratic society containing a significant number of non-Catholics cannot be expected to adhere to the norms of Catholic teaching on abortion. It may legitimately have a law permitting abortion. Though this is the logic of the Catholic position, particularly since *Evangelium Vitae*, John Paul II seems unready to accept it. He issued the encyclical to strengthen the fight against abortion but by failing to attend to the logic of his argument he here actually undermines it.

Certainly the gospel is not there to be voted on. And it is true there are risks in democracy. It can fall prey to national deception as in Nazi Germany or the delusions of a powerful group as in South Africa under apartheid. Democracy, like conscience, has to be informed and educated. It is not simply that the enforcement of high ideals by coercion of law has been tried and failed before, as in various communist states. The grounds on which democracy is to be endorsed in the political context, and yet not in the moral one, are not made clear. At the heart of the problem is the church's idea about the formation of the good Catholic citizen. When looking at the secular world he or she is supposed to be adult, active, well-informed, educated, critical of authority, sceptical, intolerant of injustice, ready to participate and take responsibility, in other words to be a certain kind of moral being. Yet when faced with papal pronouncements he or she is expected suddenly to become deferential, docile, obedient and infantile. In reality it is not possible for Catholic citizens to change into something quite different in this way. The best they can do is to pretend to be that other sort of person. But privately they will be judging those who administer the church with those same values and attributes which the church asks and expects them to have as good citizens when judging civil authority. If 'I was only obeying orders' is judged by Catholic Social Teaching not to be an acceptable excuse for failing to exercise individual responsibility in the temporal sphere, it seems implausible that it should be acceptable in matters spiritual. Beyond a certain point you cannot be a citizen of two worlds at once, if those worlds are too different.

There are other problems in addition. The possibility seems never to be contemplated by John Paul II that the basis for democracy might not be the 'right to life' but rather some other set of assumptions about the significance of humanity. Nor that there may be an argument to be had about the basis on which some Christians countenance circumstances in which abortion might be permissible, nor about those who insist that euthanasia is worse than abortion. This is not to say that the pope's position is necessarily wrong; only that there is something inconsistent about his lack of openness to others' insights and questions.

Others are working at reconciling the tension between morality and democracy in a pluralist society. 'The Church has been able to make its own contribution to political theory by exploring the limitations of the democratic process,' said the Catholic bishops of England and Wales in *The Common Good*, the document they issued before the 1997 British general election. 'Democracy can never be a self-fulfilling justification for policies that are intrinsically immoral. Democracy is not a self-sufficient moral system. Democracy, if it is to be healthy, requires more than universal suffrage: it requires the presence of a system of common values. If democracy is not to become a democratic tyranny in which the majority oppresses the minority, it is necessary for the public to have an understanding of the common good and the concepts that underlie it.'[18] It is in this direction that lies a future reconciliation between the demands of absolute values and the recognition that democracy is an inalienable right for human persons. Democracy – like human rights, which the church also once opposed – must now be fundamental to the Christian concept of human dignity. Because all people are made in the image of God they must be given the opportunity to make choices. That means they must be allowed the freedom to make decisions under the wider laws which pluralistic societies must have if they are to respect the diversity of opinion which exists within them. Freedom of choice is not here a consumer demand so much as a fundamental expression of the exercise of free will for which individuals will be held responsible.

When the pope states in *Tertio Millennio Adveniente* that 'it must be asked how many Christians really know and put into practice the principles of the church's social doctrine,'[19] the answer may be that Catholic Social Teaching is paradoxically referred to as the Church's Best Kept Secret because the church makes so few attempts to alter that position; go into a Catholic church any Sunday and, for all the social encyclicals, Catholic Social Teaching is rarely what you hear from the pulpit. But it may also have something to do with the inconsistency of advocating democracy in the political sphere but not permitting it in the moral one, and in the complete refusal to admit any element of democracy in the internal governance of the church itself. The suppression of what others might call disagreement but a Polish pope terms 'dissent' has already been noted. The radical steps outlined at Medellín, and endorsed by Pope Paul VI, to bring the church's governance into line with its teaching on social transformation have never been implemented. For many, questions of integrity are raised by papal re-iterations of approval for the insights of Vatican II when they are combined with a determination not to devolve much decision-making to the laity, and most especially women. The concern is not so much the venal reluctance of any group with power not to relinquish it, but that despite all its rhetoric on empowerment, there appear to be contradictions in the church's own teaching about conscience, human dignity and participation.

There is evidence that this is a serious stumbling block for some. 'The authoritarian tendency embedded in these encyclicals is problematic . . . You cannot simultaneously concede that one can learn from others and at the same time exclude any discussion or disagreements,' said one of the brightest of the new generation of moral theologians, Ian Markham, an Anglican who chose the subject of Catholic Social Teaching for his inaugural lecture[20] for the Chair of Theology and Public Life at Liverpool Hope University. His critique constituted a ringing endorsement of John Paul II's twelve encyclicals since 1979 which Markham concluded constitute a 'brilliant' and 'coherent analysis of modernity'. The pope's manifesto for the new millennium he sees as consisting of a friendly conversation with capitalism, a strong affirmation of truth in morality discovered through natural law, a passionate opposition to the 'culture of death', and a determination to encourage the universal church to work together more effectively. Markham describes this as 'a remarkable set of documents' which contain much that is self-evidently right – 'the need to make the market work on behalf of the poor, the danger of judging all human life on the basis of utility rather than intrinsic value; and the need to witness to the possibility of truth in morals, without which no civilization can survive'.[21]

Yet, he says, it has one major defect: 'it seems to me to ignore the entire revelatory significance of complexity and ambiguity . . . The complexities of modern life are not conceded: there is no dialogue with external expertise . . . As if fuelled by a fear of the whole system unravelling, the ethical task is reduced to simple uncomplicated obedience to those who know better. The experience of all those who think otherwise is simply disregarded.'²² Markham's general thesis, as set out in his book *Plurality and Christian Ethics*,²³ is that God intended the complexity and plurality of the ethical domain; theology can therefore only be effective when it takes account of the culture of the age.

To have an impact, therefore, theology must take account of the applied experience of those to whom it speaks. Points of contact must be established. Only a few of those in the world of work are wicked, corrupt or exploitative; most find themselves in situations which are confusing, ambiguous or present professional dilemmas. The church's guidance on these problems needs to be informed and take into account the complexity of the real world. To simply divide all human experience into 'good' or 'bad', or belonging to a culture of 'life' or of 'death', fails to make contact with all those situations which are in between. These problems become more pronounced when the Vatican attempts to move from broad-brush morality to engagement with the detail of a particular profession. As Markham puts it: 'We need to become much more sensitive to the ways in which good intentions have either been thwarted by institutions or have unforeseen side-effects. Public life is made of dilemmas where the right and the good are rarely clear. There is a danger that the language of morality will be confined to those who want to sloganize: to avoid that danger it is vital that the churches illustrate that moral discourse can meet people where they are.'²⁴

Globalization – an appropriate response

But there is one key area where John Paul does seem to admit some uncertainty. It was also aired at the Pontifical Academy with the revealing preamble that, of course, the church's social teaching derives from 'principles based on the natural law and the word of God' and therefore 'does not vary with the changes of history. However these principles can be constantly clarified, especially in their concrete applications.' The pope was glossing a speech he made the year before when he told the same body 'the moral principle according to which the demands of the market . . . must not go against the primordial rights of every man to have work through which he can earn a living for himself and his family'.[25] A year on, after reportedly being influenced by the right-wing American Catholic theologian, Michael Novak, he was insisting that though the welfare state has a role to play in rectifying the demands of the market it must function 'moderately' to avoid the dependency culture in which 'excessive assistance . . . creates more problems than it solves'. More than that he seemed even to be expressing ambivalence about the deregulation of the financial markets which were unleashed by the Thatcher and Reagan administrations to restore the supremacy of individual acts of choice within an untrammelled free market. Previously the pope had expressed grave reservations about such policies. Now he was saying 'the church does not mean to condemn the deregulation of the market itself, but asks that it be envisaged and implemented with respect for the primacy of the human person.'[26]

The pope's equivocation here is perhaps a reflection of the continuing general uncertainty about the process of globalization by which the world economy is rapidly becoming ever more interdependent. Globalization has been hailed as a panacea by right-wingers and has been demonized with equal and opposite fervour by the Left. The reality is somewhat more complex. There are at least five major, interconnected, but distinct processes wrapped up inside the notion of globalization. First, over the past decade there has been a revolution in information and communications technology. Second, there has been – thanks to the reforms motivated by the *laissez-faire* ideology of the Thatcher and Reagan administrations – a massive deregulation of the way money is allowed to flow around the world. National boundaries and habits are becoming increasingly less relevant to business decisions, as investment flows and production facilities move in quest of the highest possible returns or market share. This places national economies at the mercy of multinational decision-making and foreign exchange dealers on a scale which was hitherto thought impossible, as was demonstrated in the breaching of the European Exchange Rate Mechanism in 1992 despite its backing by the combined weight of

Europe's most powerful governments. Third, the production and distribution of goods across the world has become increasingly interdependent and even integrated. Fourth, there has been a significant burgeoning of trade, particularly in the service sector. And finally there has been continuing growth in the importance of large mainly multinational companies.

There can be no doubt that the enormous increase in economic productivity of the end of this century has meant that a wider range of people have access to a wider range of goods. It has meant greater choice, the conquest of many diseases and enhanced life spans for millions. But it still has the perennial boom-or-bust feature of capitalist dynamics with periods of growth followed in cycle by others of recession. And the creation of wealth is parallelled by the generation of inequality poverty, and suffering. If globalization creates greater wealth, it will also create greater disparities, within and between nations. Some Third World nations, notably the 'tiger' economies of the Far East, have turned some of these developments to their advantage; but most have simply fallen further behind creating serious new difficulties for the Third World. Two-thirds of the world's population is now virtually written off as far as foreign investment is concerned. Few mainstream economists now believe there is much scope for poor nations to opt out of the world economy and yet flows of investment cash largely pass them by. Through the strategies of globalization, the flow of foreign direct investment, and the introduction of these new technologies, multinational companies are creating global overcapacity in industry after industry. New types of frictions between nations and trading blocks – the European Union, the North American Free Trade Area Agreement (NAFTA) and the emerging Asian and Latin American blocks – will be the consequence as the world adjusts to these changed conditions and as the workers of the West find themselves in ever increased competition with the cheap labour of the Third World. The poor of the Third World are in a much weaker position to respond than are European trade unions who themselves have proved largely powerless.

Power, as much as economics, is at the heart of the problem here. Globalization, which its advocates trumpet as the way to achieve optimal outcomes for growth and human welfare, is far from raising the standards of all in the slipstream of greater wealth for the rich. All vessels will rise on a rising economic tide, its proponents argue; in fact those whose boats are holed, or anchored to the sea-bed, are beginning to drown – and the prospects for the future seem worse. John Paul II, in his recent comments to the Pontifical Academy, appears acutely aware of this. Though he insists still on first dismissing the inadequacies of communism – 'history amply demonstrates the failure of regimes characterized by planning' – he moves swiftly on to the limitations of modern capitalism. 'Experience shows that a market economy, left to unconditional freedom, is far from bringing the greatest possible advantages to individuals and societies.' An unbridled market which, under the pretext of competitiveness, prospers by exploiting man and the environment to excess is 'ethically unacceptable' and can only have disastrous long-term consequences. Ethics cannot wait on economic development; they must develop in harmony. 'There are still too many people in the world who have no access to the least portion of the opulent wealth of a minority,' he says, and continues that 'the globalized organization of work, profiting from the extreme privation of developing peoples, often entails grave situations that mock the elementary demands of human dignity.' He speaks of 'the most underprivileged people crushed by the exorbitant power of the global market'.

But there is more to the problem than that. The power of unfettered markets to unravel traditional forms of social life has brought changes in the nature of work. The result is massive movements of capital, currency and now jobs from one side of the globe to the other (to wherever the greatest profit can be made) and economic changes whose impact was once cushioned by welfare and regional regeneration are now felt nakedly, as is testified by the large numbers of people made redundant as production is shifted around the globe. In the West globalization has accelerated the decline in the manufacturing industries and increased the importance of technology. All of which places new emphasis on education and is building a society which is more 'middle class' – with the exception of those who are left behind when the skills gap opens up, the so-called 'underclass', whose inactivity the Conservative Chancellor of the Exchequer Norman Lamont once so memorably said was a 'price worth paying' for low inflation. More significantly the effects of globalization have not ended there. The ill-effects have spread to the middle class who now also feel the water lapping at their feet with industrial 'down-sizing' and redundancy. It has brought with it the rise of casualization, the growth of the contract culture and the increase in part-time work. Combine this with the degradation of public services and rising crime levels and the result is that high degrees of risk and uncertainty become routine, creating a heightened sense of job insecurity and a world in which all relationships come to be perceived as revocable and transitory. Ever more demands are made for increased mobility, detaching individuals from localities and weakening commitments to families: marital breakdown is commonest in places where labour mobility and unemployment are both high. Joblessness has emasculated the power of trade unions to combat this. It is a world in which the gap between the 'haves' and 'have nots' increases. In the years between 1990 and 1995 average earnings rose by 16% in the US. But annual redundancies went up by 39%. To underscore the widening gap between the rich and the poor total corporate profits in the same period were up by 75% and chief executives' average pay went up by 92%.[27] It is a world of Social Darwinism. From a culture of contentment we have moved to a culture of resentment: those in work, work too hard, and yet are insecure; those who are without a job find themselves increasingly sentenced to long-term unemployment and dismissal as the 'underclass'.

What is needed, Pope John Paul also told the Pontifical Academy of Social Sciences, is political activity to ensure a balanced and well-regulated world market. Only that would couple prosperity with the development of culture, democracy, solidarity and peace. 'The more global the market, the more it must be balanced by a global culture of solidarity, attentive to the needs of the weakest.'[28]

Unfortunately globalization, combined with a resurgence of selfishness among nations, makes the ethical and legal regulation of the market more difficult. 'What is needed,' he concludes, 'is an increased co-ordination among the more powerful countries' – and the pope throws particular responsibility on the United Nations, International Monetary Fund and the World Trade Organisation.[29]

In a previous age his remarks might have been dismissed as unworldly. But across the globe philosophers and social scientists had begun to express new concern at the impact the new economic developments could have on social cohesion and eventually on world stability. Ours is a world which Marx would have recognized more easily than that of two decades ago, says the leading social democrat thinker Professor David Marquand.[30] The influential former right-wing intellectual, John Gray, alienated by the excesses of what he once advocated, has now written: 'The Thatcher project has certainly been exhausted, and the political energy by which it was animated in the early 1980s has evaporated, leaving only the dreary and unmeaning formulae of New Right ideology.'[31] In the United States, Frances Fukuyama, the one-time high priest of neo-liberalism, has turned his attention from exultations about the triumph of capitalism to worrying about ethics – his sequel to *The End of History* was a book called *Trust* which considered the ethical basis on which a successful market rests.[32] Even George Soros – who made a £6 billion fortune from the international financial markets and whose currency speculation forced Britain out of the European Exchange Rate Mechanism – warned early in 1997 that 'the untrammelled intensification of *laissez-faire* capitalism and the spread of market values into all areas of life is undermining social values of morality'.[33] It is, perhaps, a world which is now ready to listen as Catholic Social Teaching enters the mainstream debate.

Epilogue

Towards a New Politics: Catholic Social Teaching in a Pluralist Society

Paul Vallely

Anxieties always rise as civilizations decline, said the Protestant theologian Tillich. Today – when European domination of the world is over, America's is peaking and economic power is shifting to the Pacific Rim – there can be little doubt that a sense of dejection is evident in many sections of Western society. Widescale unemployment and a growing sense of job insecurity are only part of a feeling of pre-millennial tension. The values of the Enlightenment are under threat and the fear is being articulated within the great pluralist model itself, the United States, that its kids are growing up without spiritual values. There is a general intuition of a society, fragmenting under economic pressures and the anti-social philosophies of the market, in desperate need of rediscovering a sense of common good.

That is the challenge of the new millennium and it is one which is fast becoming the prime preoccupation of many philosophers, social scientists and politicians. In this Epilogue I want to examine some of these and consider the extent to which these secular thinkers are venturing on to territory already significantly explored by Catholic Social Teaching in the hundred years since the first papal social encyclical, *Rerum Novarum*, was published. The church's insights – about the nature of human dignity, about the principles for balancing the interests of the individual and society, and about the mechanisms through which those precepts can be applied – all have something to say to our post-Christian society as it enters the Third Millennium. I want to suggest some of the philosophical adjustments which a pluralist society must make to survive with peace and prosperity in the twenty-first century. And I want to look to the areas where the definitions of Catholic Social Teaching might be widened to assist in this process.

At the start of our century few people had many dealings with strangers. Our grandparents conducted most of their relationships with other people face to face. The change since their time would be hard for them to imagine. Today we are connected to others in a different way. Our telephone can link us with almost a billion people throughout the world. The Internet gives us the ability to shift vast amounts of information across thousands of miles in just seconds. But if our interconnectedness is greater it is also more flimsy. For these new technologies simultaneously seem to dilute our sense of obligation to those we encounter. They are only the latest in a long series of developments which have attenuated our sense of inter-dependence upon others. These influences have been religious – as long ago as the Reformation a new sense of individualism was fostered by the idea that every man and woman stood in a direct relationship with God, without need of mediation by some church hierarchy or tradition. They have been economic – the creation of the limited liability company allowed individuals to invest money in a project without risking personal bankruptcy if it went wrong: it was an engine of growth but also a source of social fragmentation allowing us to hide from the wider consequences of our actions as we demand that businesses, insurance companies and pension funds have no duty other than to maximize their return on our investments. And this century the changes have been, above all, technological. The car has made travel easier but developed the separateness of the suburb, while television and computer have offered the illusion of contact with far-off worlds whilst keeping them psychologically distant. All of which enables us to hide behind anonymity and, as one commentator has put it, to 'surround ourselves with more fleeting transactions that demand less in terms of understanding and intimacy'.[1] Today we belong to a very different world from the one predicted in the middle of the twentieth century by the French scientist-philosopher-priest

Pierre Teilhard de Chardin who imagined that technological change would interlock with human destinies to produce a spiritual progress which would end in the unity of everything with God.

Something has got out of kilter in the equation which Keynes[2] argued must be kept in balance by a good society, with economic efficiency and personal freedom being held in harmonious tension with social justice. Today efficiency and freedom increasingly eclipse that third social element to the point where our sense of community, commonweal, or the common life has become more elusive (if it is anything more than a pious aspiration or a political slogan). The primacy of efficiency and freedom were at the heart of the Thatcherite vision which so dominated the 1980s. It had power because it spoke persuasively to one source of human motivation – economic self-advancement. But it was, in that, fatally partial. 'Thatcherism was a self-undermining project,' in the words of the ex-Thatcherite philosopher John Gray:

> Those who formulated it did not perceive that the freeing of markets that drastically diminished the power of organized labour would have the unintended consequence, over time, of undermining economic security among the social groups who were Thatcherism's initial beneficiaries . . . The aspiring working class people who saw in Thatcherite policies the chance of upward social mobility into the middle classes, if they were successful in making the transition, discovered that the life of Middle England had been transformed beyond recognition. They emerged not in the sunlit uplands of bourgeois security, but onto a desolate plateau of middle class pauperdom. The poignant irony of Essex man and woman struggling up the economic escalator only to meet the bedraggled figures of the professional middle classes staggering down is a narrative of our times that has yet to be fully chronicled.[3]

It brought with it, as the Chief Rabbi, Jonathan Sacks has noted, the fragmentation of culture, the collapse of the family, the ghettoization of cities, the loss of a sense of continuity with the past and a culture of the individual with no larger loyalties than personal choice and provisional contracts.[4]

There are inherent tendencies in our post-modern societies to deplete the common moral culture. The unintended consequence of neo-liberal deregulation of markets – and what Pope John Paul II has called the 'powerful cultural, economic and political currents which encourage an idea of society excessively concerned with efficiency'[5] – was to accelerate all these. 'In the end there is no such thing as the free market, but rather a variety of cultural institutions and legal devices and instruments through which economic life is mediated,' the apostate Gray was forced to conclude, conceding that in the decade before neo-liberals like him had neglected the cultural matrices of economic life. Market freedoms, he now insists, are only a means to an end. That end is individual well-being. Yet individual well-being requires certain forms of common life. And these the market undermines. 'Market institutions are not free-standing,' says Gray, 'but come embedded in the matrices of particular cultures and their histories.' And some goods – like healthcare and educational opportunity – ought to be distributed according to ethical rather than economic criteria – that is to say, on the basis of need rather than the ability to pay. 'The over-riding task we confront today,' Gray concludes, 'is that of preserving, and extending, forms of common life which highly individualist market institutions threaten to undermine or corrode . . . . Individual autonomy presupposes a strong public culture in which choice and responsibility go together as part of a common good.'[6]

The response of traditionalists here is to try to find a way of coming to terms with the contradiction which arises from trying to support, on the one hand, both deregulated markets and, on the other, inherited cultural traditions, allegiances and hierarchical forms of social order. It was a reconciliation which, in Britain, the Conservative Party tried unsuccessfully to affect in the dying years of Thatcherism under John Major. And yet if that did not work neither can a return to the old formularies of the post-war consensus of social democracy. The old prescriptions of social democracy are problematic, resting as they did on the notion of full employment and a cradle-to-grave welfare state. Those were days of full male employment, stable nuclear families and low female employment. The welfare state has found it difficult to adapt to a world of long-term male unemployment, rising rates of divorce, and high female participation in the labour force. More than that the welfare state has proved very expensive. In Britain today social security, health and education together account for 60% of government spending; this welfare state absorbs all the revenue raised by our four largest taxes – income tax, national insurance, VAT and corporation tax. The attempts of the last Conservative government to cut back public spending foundered on this rock. Despite the sharp cuts in real terms on health, education, defence, justice, arts and transport, almost all the savings were absorbed – thanks to the rise in unemployment – by a dramatic rise in spending on social security benefits. Today between a third and a quarter of families with children in the UK live below the official poverty line and receive state benefits. In the future this crisis can only grow with the increasing numbers of elderly, unemployed, lone parents and long-term sick. And it can only be further exacerbated by our growing appetite for the improvements in health and education provision which technology has produced. It is a problem which is facing not just Britain but the whole of the Western world.

The old solutions involved either hefty tax-and-spend policies or massive government borrowing on the model advocated by Keynes.[7] The first option is impossible because taxpayers seem unwilling to finance such spending, and show no sign of changing so long as modern democracy avoids confronting people with problems in the belief that any political party which does so is doomed to defeat (a process which insidiously robs us each of a proper sense of individual responsibility). The second option is ruled out by the new global freedom of capital which, since the deregulation of the Thatcher/Reagan era, has severely limited the room for manoeuvre of governments. Growing the welfare state – to meet the higher-than-inflation demands of health and education

– is unsustainable when the power of international currency and bond markets is such that they can stop governments borrowing as Keynes proposed. Promoting full employment through borrowing is similarly constrained. In France, the Mitterand regime tried it in the early 1980s without success, and earlier this decade the Swedish model collapsed for the same reasons. Elsewhere the European social democratic economic model appears to be in long-term retreat and unable to find a solution to the central problem of mass structural unemployment. Likewise using the tax system to promote goals of wealth distribution is severely constrained by the international mobility of capital and people. And the forces behind globalization have all but emasculated the power of trade unions. 'Global freedom of capital,' as John Gray puts it, 'effectively demolishes the economic foundations of social democracy.'[8] The next generation of politicians, like Tony Blair, have begun to talk about a 'Third Way', though they seem no clearer than anyone else as to what this might actually be.

The search for a secular morality

In any case, there is a more fundamental problem. The old foundations of liberalism, on which more than a century of social progress has been built, are now showing signs of collapsing under their own contradictions. By liberalism I mean the idea, which has its roots in the eighteenth-century Enlightenment, that all beliefs should be tolerated so long as they are not anti-social. The notion sounds tolerant and fair and is superficially attractive. But, in the end, it is not enough.

Up to a point it has served us well. A century of religious wars had preceded the Enlightenment when it jettisoned authoritarian religious orthodoxy and replaced it with an approach of rational scientific inquiry. Since then the Western world has embraced scepticism, individualism and traditionless rationality. Church and state were separated, and the freedom and tolerance enshrined by the new secularism freed the energies which produced the industrial revolution, the modern democratic state and a high culture of science, art and learning. But it had limitations. Its enthusiasms for science brought great technological progress but also an arms race and environmental pollution on a devastating scale. Its privatization of morality furthered freedom and choice, but in doing so it has created a supermarket of values from which everyone chooses just whatever suits them. Most profoundly, its emphasis upon individual self-interest created *homo oeconomicus* – men and women obsessed with the creation of wealth and apparently oblivious to the atomizing effect this had on society.

It is only now that we are coming to realize the extent to which the subversive dynamism of market forces has inexorably dissolved the framework of personal relationships in families and communities – and the rules, rituals and traditions which sustain them – which give meaning to life. On top of that liberal secularism has also devalued cultural, linguistic, ethnic and religious diversity and eroded the communities and institutions in which peoples found common purpose. The combined result has been, as the Chief Rabbi has put it, that today modern individuals have 'no larger loyalties than personal choice and provisional contracts'.[9] Modern man, confined to the language of individualism, has lost the ability to make moral sense of his life and taken refuge in a worldview which celebrates consumerism, the freedom of the individual and a blind faith in science. Its ideology is post-modernism in that it rejects the hegemony of any one tradition within our culture and insists that the quest for a universal narrative is over. Its philosophy deems society as little more than a space in which conflicts are fought out, with employers and employees, ethnic and religious communities, single issue pressure groups and a host of others all pressing their disparate claims on the state – a state which increasingly seems to lack the core of shared values it needs to adjudicate on disputes between these different groups of people.

Once religion provided those common values. There was not necessarily anything spiritual in them. Religion has always been seen by some as a useful mechanism of social control. The various modes of worship in the Roman world, as Gibbon tells us, were all considered by the people as equally true, by the philosopher as equally false and by the magistrate as equally useful. And even as quintessential an Enlightenment figure as Voltaire declared that he wanted his attorney, tailor, servants and even his wife to believe in God, so he should be robbed and cuckolded less often. But the story of the twentieth century, in the West, has been one of the decline of religion and the self-confident rise of secular humanism and the gradual depletion of the centuries' accumulation of Judaeo-Christian moral capital. And, as the philosopher Alasdair MacIntyre says in *After Virtue*, the language of morality disintegrates when it is disentangled from the religious context which was its source and made it intelligible.[10]

Secular liberalism, it seems, has no source from which to replenish this moral capital. The offspring of the Enlightenment – science, capitalism, individualism and democracy – are all enabling mechanisms but none of them contain values. They are what MacIntyre has called 'second order moralities': they create a framework within which other virtues can flourish, but they do not provide those values. Not to recognize this is to elevate pluralism into an ideology. It leads us without a map into a world of amorality in which capitalists will do almost anything to make money, scientists will acknowledge no limits on where they may push the bounds of technological achievement and democrats drift into a relativism in which morality is simply a way of expressing preferences. The empty husk of liberal tolerance has little to offer a society which needs to find mechanisms to regenerate personal responsibility, a sense of community and end the marginalization or exclusion of the unskilled and alienated it brands the 'underclass'.

But morality is not one human enterprise among others, says Jonathan Sacks. 'It is the base which makes other enterprises possible and the vantage point from which they are judged.' Moralities are like languages, we do not invent them by our individual choices. Like languages they must be learned. 'By learning them we take part in a particular tradition which long preceded us. They tell us that there are some rules whose claim upon us is stronger than short-term self-interest and involve a commitment to the institutions into which we were born and from which our identity derives.'[11]

So how are we to counter the tendencies inherent in late modern societies to deplete the common moral culture – a process which the neo-liberal deregulation of markets and of capital has only accelerated? How, in a multi-cultural and multi-faith society, can we arrive at a common position which can be shared by people with very different substantive moral outlooks? For, without that, society will not have the base from which to work out a solution to the central dilemma of our time: how accelerating changes in technology and the economy are to be reconciled with the abiding human need for stability and for forms of the common life.

The task is now exercising many contemporary thinkers outside the churches. The idea that everything should be for sale was challenged some time ago by the philosopher Michael Walzer who illustrated that we can only do that at the cost of disregarding real values. If we attend to those values, there are things which cannot be bought and sold. Most societies block some commercial transactions. These 'blocked exchanges', as he calls them, include things like: selling votes for cash or favours; buying political office; bribing a judge; profiteering in war or famine; or producing unsafe goods. In such cases society says these are social values which must be defended against the market.[12] The problem is, how do we differentiate between what can be bought and what ought not to be?

There have been attempts by thinkers such as the American social scientist Amitai Etzioni to define 'community' as the third apex to the triangle of values alongside individual freedom and economic efficiency. The prescriptions of such communitarians have proved problematic. They range from the authoritarian to the merely platitudinous. Etzioni has a number of coercive elements in his vision: he favours national service, compulsory organ donation, random breath tests for drivers and public humiliation of criminals as an alternative to prison. Others, like Jonathan Sacks, are more hortative. Community, he says, is 'any voluntary organization of people larger than the individual and smaller than the state'.[13]

Presumably he means by that religious associations, trade unions, businessmen's clubs, charities, pressure groups, residents' associations, parent-teacher committees, local history societies and even the Neighbourhood Watch – all the countless little platoons which Edmund Burke spoke about as making up British society and which give the lie to the notion that society is, as Hobbes put it, a mere association set up to maintain order. To the Chief Rabbi this society offers a vision of Britain as a 'community of communities'.

But putting flesh on the bones of such a vision is a more difficult task. Two antagonistic principles dominate modern life, according to Geoff Mulgan, founder of the think-tank Demos and a senior policy advisor to the British Prime Minister Tony Blair.[14] They are that of the growing reality of interdependence and the continuing urge for personal freedom which shows no sign of diminishing. The new interdependence is manifested in everything from our new consciousness of ecology – so that our choice to drive a car or to dump waste impacts swiftly on others – to the reality of a global economy which makes the livelihood of a town in north-east England dependent on capital from Korea and markets in Germany. But, as he says, this 'interweaving of connections has coincided with the rise in a culture in which individual freedom is valued above all else . . . Coming after centuries and millennia in which most people were held down by oppressive hierarchies, it is not surprising that freedom is valued so highly. But now we confront a difficult question: whether the achievement of new freedoms is really compatible with the growth of interdependence?'[15] Clearly he feels the answer must be 'No' in a world which devotes so much energy to the pursuit of individual desires that the thirst for total freedom can become a pathology. For freedom must entail the opportunity to leave the family or community, to act against its interests, he concludes. And this excessive individualism creates direct costs for society:

> For many the right to break away from an unhappy marriage was a great advance, but freedom in family life leaves huge costs in its wake. Today in the UK and the USA nearly half of all

marriages end in divorce. Millions of children suffer from the deficit of parental attention that tends to result if parents value their own careers and pleasures more than their responsibilities to their children. Much the same could be said of the relationship between employers and employees . . . In a fluid and open market the pressures seem to make employers more casual in their treatment of staff, and employees less willing to make any commitments back: both see their relationship in short-term instrumental fashion . . . It costs more if everyone travels in a private car and is willing to spend long spells in traffic jams; more if everyone choses to live alone or to live in a house large enough to accommodate the children of a previous marriage at weekends; more if people have to protect themselves against the actions of others that in another society might be held in check by mutual moral suasion.[16]

Yet comprehending the facts will not be sufficient to make people more tolerant, responsible or understanding. The difficulty of adapting to this more brittle society, and to the fragile ecology in which we now understand it exists, will require a change in structures but also in mentality. Mulgan talks of social orders which are less authoritarian and hierarchical than of old and which are, instead, more reciprocal, transparent and based on dialogue. But he also talks of sacrifice in changes to personal and industrial lifestyles, particularly among the rich nations.

Another Demos thinker, Charles Leadbeater, goes a step further. He tries to discover mechanisms whereby this new sense of Civic Spirit, as he calls it, might be cultivated. He, too, starts from a similar position, seeing 'the threads of society are being pulled apart by a gale of economic restructuring and eaten away by individualism'.[17] We have lost faith in institutions – the monarchy, church, the traditional family – which no longer seem able to do their jobs; we retain faith in those which do – the market and private companies. The task now is to transfer the qualities and mechanisms of the successful institutions to the unsuccessful ones. That will mean finding a new balance between justice, decency, community and choice. Justice, he says, must link rewards to performance, skill and effort. Decency protects people's self-respect in a way communist bloc societies never could. Community means we must, once again, begin to care about how people behave in public spaces: we have to abandon the 'anything goes' liberalism which is to retreat from judgment where in fact we ought to promote a sense of belonging. Choice means harnessing the force of the striving, choosing individual but nurturing a 'broader, more engaged, more creative individualism which promotes both autonomy and responsibility'.

How is all this to be done? Leadbeater's chosen mechanism is the re-establishment of the mutual societies which, before the advent of the welfare state, provided health, insurance and banking services. His model is the club. Clubs are hybrids, he says, blurring the line between ownership and consumption. They centre around the principle of mutuality. At their core is the idea of reciprocity. Membership is earned: you have to put in before you take out. Within them rights also bring obligations. Shared investments yield shared gains. They have built-in learning mechanisms: because members both provide the service and also use it, clubs translate consumer ideas quickly into practice. Clubs also inspire a sense of belonging and loyalty. They are the paradigm of what a post-modern society needs. Dismissing the fact that many of the mutual societies – in banking and insurance – have in recent years transformed themselves into limited companies to raise more capital for growth, Leadbeater predicts a future in which mutual societies provide education, health, insurance, housing and even policing alongside private companies and the state. Society needs to invest in public institutions which are capable of reconciling the diverse and conflicting identities thrown up by a pluralist society.

The moral compass of Catholic Social Teaching

What will be evident from all this is the extent to which secular thinkers are reaching tentatively out into the terrain which Catholic Social Teaching has charted so throughly over the past century, with each generation building upon the insights of its predecessors, re-interpreting that tradition through the changing needs of the times. Catholic notions about the nature of human dignity, the common good, subsidiarity, solidarity and structural sin may well constitute the compass which our post-modern society needs as it sets out on its journey into the next millennium.

• Its doctrine on human dignity has important insights about how the rights of individuals are intrinsic; they do not stem from some social compact and thus cannot be alienated or abrogated – and nor can a philosophy of relativism alter them according to some utilitarian calculus. It is from this that stems the right of all to basic living standards, including education and employment. There is a right and a duty to work, for work in its fullest sense is what makes us fully human.

• Its doctrine on the common good speaks to the social dimension which is essential to human flourishing; the family is an important part of this but the insight goes wider. The common good requires a balance between the rights of the individual and the wider good of society. It insists that all have the right, and demands that all must have the political and economic wherewithal, to participate fully in that society. Its notion of integral human development requires that no one should be excluded from the benefits of social development This means that authority may have to lean towards the interests of the weakest and most vulnerable. Some re-distribution of wealth is to be required. The contemporary over-emphasis upon the rights of the individual violates the common good, as does the modern over-emphasis of economic efficiency and profit. The market must be a tool not an ideology, and the state has a role to play, nationally and internationally, in regulating that market.

• Its doctrine of subsidiarity requires that the state should not take upon itself what individuals can do; but it also requires that the state should not shirk from doing what it can do better than individuals or private bodies – issues concerning the environment or the regulation of international finance and trade are obvious examples. It maintains that workers have a right to join trade unions. Its doctrine of solidarity insists that interdependence is a moral issue; that rich individuals and nations have a duty to help the poor; that everyone has a responsibility to commit themselves to the common good. Its doctrine of structural sin – with its insight that sin can reside in social and economic structures and institutions as well as in the acts of individuals – casts a searching light upon much activity of which the mechanisms of the market wash their hands. It asserts through the notion of the indirect employer that anyone who benefits from exploitation – knowingly or not – has moral culpability for it.

So where do the principles of Catholic Social Teaching point for the future? They suggest a need to rebalance our political programmes on both the domestic and international fronts. Some of the broad-brush changes needed are self-evident. The imperatives of the bias to the poor are straightforward. So are those which point to a more inclusive society in which all are empowered and encouraged to participate. Subsidiarity requires greater participation in the processes of government in ways which give ordinary people greater say in their lives; the common good requires more transparency in government to enable greater accountability; solidarity insists on effective safety nets for the disadvantaged, though subsidiarity insists that these must not create disincentives to work.

But Catholic Social Teaching also has insights to offer into specific areas of policy. Creating full employment through government borrowing and spending on public works, as Keynes advocated, may now be circumscribed by the influence of the deregulated markets, but nonetheless the church's teaching on work has something to say to a modern finance minister. Because work for all is a social good as well as the right and duty of each individual, it is unethical that governments in the past have used unemployment as a tool to control inflation, with the benefit for the many falling as a disproportionate burden on the shoulders of an unfortunate few. Unemployment on the scale we have seen in Britain over the past decade is not an economic inevitability; other economies, like that of the United States, have made full employment one of the primary goals of the strategy of both government and the US Federal Reserve, its equivalent of the Bank of England. Countering the social exclusion created by unemployment is, then, a primary task: the imperatives of the common good, solidarity and subsidiarity combine most fundamentally to demand a return to an economic and fiscal strategy which puts employment at the top of the contemporary agenda.

Nor can that be done by endorsing wages so low that workers find it difficult to live. Once economists associated poverty, in the developed nations, with unemployment. But in the last decade it is becoming associated as much with low pay – what Bishop David Sheppard has called 'humiliatingly low pay'[18] – in a way which was previously typical only of the Third World. Catholic Social Teaching draws here on the mediaeval concept of a 'just wage', one which allows the worker to sustain a minimum standard of living, meagre but decent. Of course the Middle Ages were a very different time, one of coherence and cohesion. Society then was one in which everyone knew his or her place and most people were kept firmly in theirs. It was a time when the idea of a 'just wage' or a 'just price' was more easily comprehended than is possible in an age whose thinking is dominated by the 'flexibility' of free market capitalism with its cycles of boom and boost. But even if the notion becomes harder to pin down in a globalized market economy – and in households where there are two wage-earners – there are still boundaries which, if transgressed, violate a sense of justice. Where wages do fall below the level necessary for maintaining an appropriate standard of living, the state may step in and fix by law an acceptable minimum wage. The levels at which such a minimum is fixed may be a matter for fine political judgment, but arguments for some minimum which accords with basic decency are persuasive. For there is an issue of human dignity here too, on which the principle of the common good speaks authoritatively.

To some extent the setting of a minimum wage is a useful

corrective to the reduction in the ability of ordinary working people to influence the market through trade unions. It goes some way towards the common good requirement that a balance is created between the ability of business to create wealth and the rights of individual working people not be exploited or treated callously. But the right to come together in trade unions is a fundamental right here which Catholic Social Teaching firmly, if unfashionably, upholds. The history of recent decades has shown that such a right can be abused, as where union members use their power to blackmail the rest of society or to advance their interests against those of lower-paid workers who lack their industrial muscle. But if the union reforms introduced in the UK by Margaret Thatcher were necessary correctives, there are indications that, with the deunionization brought about by globalization, the balance has shifted too far and that some union rights may be in need of restoration. Again this is a matter for fine political judgment rather than ideology.

On welfare policy, too, Catholic Social Teaching has insights. Subsidiarity demands that individuals have the duty to work, but solidarity insists also on the duty of others to ensure that those deprived of work through no fault of their own are afforded a certain basic standard of living. There is an ambiguity here, as was expressed by John Paul II when he spoke of 'the moral principle according to which the demands of the market . . . must not go against the primordial rights of every man to have work' and then warned in the same speech that the welfare state must function 'moderately' to avoid the dependency culture in which 'excessive assistance . . . creates more problems than it solves'. To be sure there is a tension here, but the concept of solidarity does not exclude opposition and confrontation, indeed it sometimes demands them. The common good requires an accommodation between these two necessities which will ratchet standards up rather than driving them down.

But there is another area of welfare policy where the church's thinking is pertinent. Through work the human person shares in the making of the world; as John Paul II asserts 'the basis for determining the value of human work is not primarily the kind of work being done but the fact that the one who is doing it is a person'.[19] By which he does not mean that all work is dignified by human involvement. Degrading work does exactly the opposite. But rather he means we should be looking for value in a wider range of qualities, so that, say, an imperfect object made by a handicapped person does have greater intrinsic value than a superficially superior one made by mass-production methods. In recent decades our society has slipped into a Hobbsean view of the poor and others whom it alienates or excludes. Poverty today is not seen as a moral problem for society but an economic one to be considered in terms of its social consequences: to secure the peaceful functioning of capitalism the casualties of the economy should be taken care of. Welfare programmes have become a mechanism for attaining social, rather than individual, good. Thinking about welfare has largely lost the sense of the intrinsic worth of the individuals who find themselves dependent upon social assistance. Calculations about welfare budgets have become mere cost-benefit analyses about whether the cost of welfare outweighs the social costs of neglect. In welfare our values have ceased to be transcendent and become utilitarian. Such a value shift imperceptibly alters society's attitudes to the individuals caught in our poverty traps and we begin to treat them differently. Such thinking has implications for the kind of welfare-to-work programmes Catholic Social Teaching might endorse but also requires us perhaps to widen our definitions of what constitutes 'work' so that we might include voluntary, charitable or caring activities which existing social security regulations exclude.

The common good speaks powerfully to the modern business community too. It endorses the concept of 'stakeholding' which certain sections of the commercial world have developed in recent years. By contrast with shareholders – those who have capital tied up in the fortunes of a firm – stakeholders covers all those with whom a business relates: shareholders, management, staff, customers, suppliers and those who live in the area in which it operates or are affected by its activities in any way. The notion, which originated in the United States, offers a useful corrective to some of the automatic assumptions of old-style *laissez-faire* capitalism. The free market may be the natural way in which human beings do business with one another, but there is nothing natural or inevitable about certain of the mechanisms of capitalism. The market may be a default mechanism but the framework in which it exists, and tools like the limited company, are culturally determined. Limited liability may have promoted wealth-creating risk-taking, but its single focus has had a down-side. We have elevated the return we expect on investments above all considerations of the impact that may have on our broader needs so that, for example, our pension fund may maximize its profits by withdrawing investments from the company in which we work, throwing us out of a job and yet leaving us with no means to countermand the decision. Catholic Social Teaching insists that limited liability has a corollary – social responsibility. Otherwise corporations are free riders on the moral, social and environmental fabric. Increasingly this is recognized as is evident from the burgeoning of a sense of 'corporate responsibility', most specifically in the US, by which business have come to accept a greater sense of obligation towards wider society prompting the growth of social activities which go far beyond the idea that it is merely good PR for a firm to involve itself with charitable and community activity. Rather they stem from the idea that a company, if it is to prosper, will best do so within the framework of a society which is just and orderly.

To make such a notion more than a pious aspiration a mechanism is being devised to monitor it. Modelled on the principle of financial accounting and auditing, systems of social accounting and auditing have been developed. Pioneered in the UK by bodies like Traidcraft Exchange and the New Economics Foundation,[20] social accounting is now being explored by a number of major British businesses to measure the impact that their trading has on staff and their families, their suppliers and customers, the area in which they operate and the physical environment which their work effects. It is a device which enables the requirements of solidarity and subsidiarity to be kept in balance. Such methods allow wider society to hold companies accountable for their activities, increasing the scope for the hitherto individualistic effects of consumerism to be harnessed in the interests of social good.

Ethical consumerism is one of the tools by which individuals can exert the pressure to make Western businesses and consumers face up to the responsibilities which are implicit in their role as indirect employer. Where in the past activists tried to exert pressure through boycotts of 'bad' companies,[21] ethical consumerism tries to favour those companies whose adoption of social accounting shows a commitment to improvements in corporate responsibility. It can make consumers' economic votes count by purchasing from companies who have agreed an approved code of conduct on the working conditions of their employees. It can purchase direct from alternative companies committed to fairer trading practices with the Third World like Traidcraft, Oxfam Trading, Equal Exchange or Twin Trading. In ordinary supermarkets it can buy products which bear the Fair Trade Mark or which are produced by companies which have adopted codes of conduct which have been endorsed by development agencies or environmental groups.[22]

The bias against the poor

But there is more than a national agenda here. The dynamics between subsidiarity and solidarity, and the option for the poor, in building the common good hold true just as much in the international arena. Indeed the need to find new mechanisms to allow the market to operate for the common good, rather than against it, are nowhere more clear than in considering the needs of the world's poorest people. The models of development which the First World has imposed upon the Third in recent decades have not been in accord with the standards of Catholic Social Teaching. The international trading system is biased against the poor rather than in favour of them. Attempts to reform it through the trade negotiations of the General Agreement on Tariffs and Trade (GATT) and its successor the World Trade Organisation (WTO) continue to exhibit a bias to the rich. Third World Debt has been used as a tool to force developing countries to toe the line with policies which, in practice, favour the interests of the rich world over the poor: arguments that the wealth of the rich would 'trickle down' have proved false as the gap between rich and poor – within nations and globally – has widened under the neo-liberal orthodoxy.

A number of key changes are needed here. Third World Debt represents a crushing hindrance to the growth of self-sufficiency which increased international trade could bring to the poor. Yet of all the handicaps they suffer it would be the easiest to remedy; effective debt relief to the twenty most needy countries[23] would cost less than the price of one Stealth bomber. There are other equally urgent action points. There is a need to reverse the drastic decline in overseas aid which has occurred throughout the Western world over the past decade. The industrialized economies also need to put an end to the barriers and quotas they impose on the import of manufactured goods from the Third World, discouraging the growth of industry there; one of the top priorities must be the reform of Europe's Common Agricultural Policy. They need also to address some of the terms of the Multilateral Agreement on Investment (MAI) which the rich nations have negotiated behind the backs of the under-developed countries and which will remove from them the legal ability to impose any controls of the activities of multinational companies. There is an equally urgent need to modify the economic adjustment packages imposed on poor countries at the behest of the International Monetary Fund so that they do not fall unduly on the poorest and weakest through health and education cuts. Indeed the great economic success stories of the last decade have not come from those countries which followed the IMF's neo-liberal formula, but rather from the 'tiger economies' of the Far East which – because they were seen as buffer states against the advance of communism – were allowed to invest heavily in health, education and skill-training against a background of land reform and the selective protection of infant industries. The result of all of that was a dynamic interaction between states and markets that, despite the severe recession which hit them in 1998, marks them out as the economic powerhouses of the future. Africa needs some of that.

Action is also needed to address the unhealthy reliance of Third World countries on primary commodities whose prices have fallen dramatically in the past twenty years. According to the World Bank, the price of commodities has halved since 1980.[24] Products like coffee and cocoa now fetch barely a quarter of what they did then. The reasons for this are complex: recession in the West which slowed the requirement for raw materials, the inability of poor farmers to respond to sudden boom-bust variations in demand, synthetic substitutes produced by new technology, competition from heavily-subsidized agricultural production in the European Union and United States, and pressure from the World Bank and IMF to grow ever more of the same produce in the mistaken assurance that commodity prices would rise during the 1980s. But the West has shown no inclination to help the Third World diversify out of its dependence on products which once produced half its income and which now produces a mere 15%.[25]

Most of the money which is made from trading in commodities does not, in any case, go to the poor. Some 95% of the deals done on the commodity futures markets do not involve the delivery of goods. A mechanism which began, when it was launched in Chicago to stabilize farm prices over the months ahead, has become little more than a casino in which dealers gamble on future prices which bear almost no fruit for the people who harvest the goods. This is part of a wider problem in modern capitalism in which money has lost its function as the means of exchange and has become instead a commodity or, as Bishop Peter Selby has argued, a divinity.[26] This non-instrumentality of money has become one of the most powerful enemies of the common good.

Nowhere is that more clear than in the disproportionate profit which can be made from speculative spot foreign exchange transactions of the kind which produced the collapse of the European Exchange Rate Mechanism in 1992 and the collapse in the Mexican currency in 1994. The combined effect of deregulation of the financial markets, sophisticated computer programmes and ever-speedier systems of telecommunication have fundamentally shifted the balance of power between governments and speculators. Twenty years ago the daily turnover of foreign exchange dealings in the world's markets was around $1 billion and the total of governments' currency reserves was around 15% of this total; by 1997 that daily turnover was $1,500 billion and official currency reserves totalled less than 1% of this amount. Of the currency traded every day in the unregulated financial markets less than 5% is related to trade in goods and services. The other 95% is simply speculative activity as traders take advantage of exchange rate fluctuations and international interest rate differentials. This kind of financial speculation plays havoc with national budgets, economic planning and allocation of resources.

Action to dampen speculative international financial movements of the kind which have, in the past, left so many national governments at the mercy of those who profit from doing nothing more than moving large amounts of money from one place to another, is entirely feasible. A small uniform tax on foreign-exchange transactions should be introduced. This Tobin Tax – named after the man who proposed it[27] – would fall heavily on money sent with lightening speed around the world to take speculative profits at various financial centres, yet it would affect long-term flows linked to trade and investments only marginally. Not only would it dampen speculation but it would also produce substantial revenues. In the developed countries that would reduce the deflationary pressures associated with cuts in public spending and provide resources for investment in a return to increased employment. For the undeveloped countries it would provide much-needed finance for development, which would, in turn, eventually feed back to create demand and employment in the West. Some have argued that such a tax would be unenforceable,[28] but just seven leading financial centres account for 80% of global financial transactions. Agreement among the European countries, Japan and the United States could produce dramatic change and increased stability. Pressure also needs to be placed upon the same govern-

ments to examine measures to encourage transnational corporations to transfer technology to the poor world, to establish
anti-trust legislation to prevent abuse of monopoly power and to
discourage tax evasion by multinationals who under-invoice or
transfer prices between their various subsidiaries. The new World
Trade Organisation could have a key role here.

At the heart of such strategies is a need to redefine what we mean
by economic efficiency. It is in considering the relationships
between the rich and poor worlds that many of the false predicates
of our definition of economic efficiency are thrown into their
starkest relief and exposed as incompatible with the trinity of solidarity, subsidiarity and the common good. Much of our modern
efficiency is limited and partial. I came across a particularly
ghastly example of this in Ethiopia in 1984. Though there was
plenty of food available in the country there was also a famine,
largely in the north where drought had dramatically reduced the
buying power of the poor. Because the people could not afford to
buy, the market shipped the food away to other areas where
purchasers did have the necessary cash. The markets worked
efficiently: the resources were automatically transferred to an area
where demand was backed by the ability to pay. As a result as many
as a million people died. Clearly the efficiency of the market here is
working in direct opposition to the creation ordinance that food
and clothing are a right for all people. Or as Tawney put it: 'To
convert efficiency from an instrument to a primary object is to
destroy efficiency itself.'[29] This is not an isolated example of evil in
efficiency. War, theft, murder, and colonialism can all be efficient
for the ruthless, but for the rest of us there is a wider moral
concern in which such efficiency must be set. Slavery was efficient
for those who were not subjugated but in the end the solution was
not for the rich to become kinder slave masters but rather to
abolish slavery. Manufacturing processes which endanger the
health of those who produce them – using asbestos or carcinogenic
paints – may be cheaper than safe alternatives but civilized societies
have quite rightly legislated against them. Other aspects of
'efficiency' need also to be questioned. Even today, when ecological

awareness is increasing, some manufacturing processes are counted as 'efficient' even though they have hidden costs which are borne by the rest of society – and its yet unborn children – in the form of environmental pollution. So a system cannot be deemed efficient if it merely improves the lot of a particular section of global society. National wealth, as we came to realize in the post-Thatcher years, is not the same as national well-being.

A dialogue for the twenty-first century

All of this is only a starting point. The raft of principles which constitute Catholic Social Teaching may, as Pope John Paul II has put it, 'be constantly clarified, especially in their concrete applications'.[30] Other interpretations than mine may be possible on the issues discussed above. In any case our society is a pluralist one, with many cultures and faiths, and if Catholic Social Teaching has something to offer to its search to re-engender a sense of common values and common purpose, it will be in a dialogue. In the journey towards a new politics for the twenty-first century the discourse will inevitably be two-way. The church has a recognition of such dialectic. 'In the history of the church, the "old" and the "new" are always closely interwoven,' John Paul II says in *Tertio Millennio Adveniente*. 'The "new" grows out of the "old," and the "old" finds a fuller expression in the "new". Thus it was for the Second Vatican Council and for the activity of the popes connected with the council, starting with John XXIII, continuing with Paul VI and John Paul I, up to the present pope.'[31] The idea is not new. Dietrich Bonhoeffer fifty years ago suggested that there may be new ideas in the secular world view which are implicitly profoundly religious, and certainly concepts like human rights, democracy and the liberation of women were formulated in secular discourse before they were taken into the theological corpus. Doubtless, some members of the church may not like the compromises which might ensue. The debate on democracy, for reasons discussed in the last chapter, will inevitably move on to territory which would have made John Paul II uncomfortable. So will the debate on the family.

The important thing here will be to distinguish values from the mere structures which have previously carried them. Fundamentalists will insist – as the ayatollahs did in Iran and the Taliban in Afghanistan – that there are some structures we have to hang on to. In the West too there is a culturally fundamentalist project among part of the New Right which wants a return to 'traditional values'. It seeks to buttress the institutions of the unfettered free market with restored forms of traditional family life. On the right politicians like John Redwood and on the left ethical socialists like Norman Dennis seek to revive vanished forms of family life. Illegitimacy, not unemployment, is the social indicator which most closely shadows the crime figure, they say, and demand that we bring back stigma. There will be Christians who take such a position, too, despite evidence that many of our traditional family mores are far more recent and culturally specific to the Victorian era than is generally assumed.[32]

Such a project does not only work against the grain of contemporary culture. The changed economic position of women, and the related issue of personal fulfilment, is one of those areas where secular trends seem utterly consonant with, if not a requirement of, Catholic Social Teaching. A revival of the 'traditional' form of family life is as unlikely as a reconstitution of the Beveridge welfare state which was based on assumptions about full male employment and low female employment. Indeed contemporary culture has already made this judgment by widening definitions of the family to include single mothers and even gay couples. A commitment to the family – in all its diverse forms – seems likely to be one of the priorities of a pluralist state.

Yet if we are about preserving values rather than structures we have to ask questions about what we mean by a family and what makes it function. Traditionally a family is, according to the Oxford English Dictionary, 'a set of parents and children, or of relations, living together or not; the unity formed by those who are nearly connected by blood or affinity; the body of persons who live in one house or under one head, including parents, children, servants, etc.'. But what are the values which distinguish a family?

'I don't know of any family in the land where they sit around the table and carve the chicken and hold up a drumstick and say: "What am I bid for this?"' So says Professor Edgar Cahn,[33] who teaches the Law and Justice course at the District of Columbia law school in Washington and is the inventor of Time Dollars – a system in which members of a local community put in an hour's work when they can, and request an hour of another member's time when they need it. Because the calculus of his system was time rather than money, the distorting effect of the market system is not replicated and tasks like caring for children, the elderly, the sick and the disadvantaged are not undervalued as they are in the market place. Cahn was originally afraid that his peers would dismiss his system as communist. So he argued: 'Well, the family is not communist but it doesn't work like the market', and then went on to offer the vivid illustration of the auction of the chicken leg at the family dinner table. The dynamics of a family, Cahn concluded, are dictated partly by shared history and interests, partly by a recognition of its members' different needs at any given time, and partly by an acknowledgment of the differing contribution of each member.

How, he then asked, could that be used more widely? 'We have an economic system that values things in a way which deep-down we don't entirely agree with. Money has replaced trust as a way of communicating and often has a toxic effect on neighbourhoods and communities,' Cahn says. What his system does is enable human beings for whom the market has no use to redefine themselves as contributors. In this way society shows it does value activities the market ignores or scorns. It redefines work and generates the social capital, an hour at a time, which is essential to rebuilding community, revitalizing neighbourhoods or strengthening families. It nurtures reciprocity and affirms self-worth. It shifts the emphasis from rights to powers, from entitlements based on status to entitlements based on contributions. It helps disadvantaged people find paths out of poverty.

If a pluralist society is to re-define the family by saying that it is a group where such self-sacrifice, love, giving, and compromise are to be found, it might also use this to discover a paradigm for the other groups which it choses to nurture in wider society. These might be the willingness to forego personal advantage for the sake of the group; the idea that because we are different we each have strengths that others need and weaknesses that others can remedy; the instinct that we survive on a complex interaction of fairness, merit and need bound together by a sense of mutuality; the notion that the common life is served by attaching duties to rights, obligations to choices, responsibilities to liberties. It is possible that in the twenty-first century something of the family will be taken to the community and of the community brought into the family. These are the very qualities which Jonathan Sacks seeks in 'community' and he too seeks them in the intermediate bodies between the family and the state which make up civil society. For it is in these 'that we acquire the virtues that sustain our common life: duty, honesty, service, self-sacrifice, integrity, neighbourliness, fortitude and civility. Without these, the workings of the market are too impersonal and arbitrary to sustain a sense of shared belonging.'[34] Reciprocity, trust and solidarity – qualities which cannot be experienced by the individual alone – are what separates communities from mere associations. These are the places, as Charles Leadbeater argued,[35] in which our citizens learn the mechanisms of mutuality. The task now is to empower local organizations where civic virtues are learned. There is something spiritual and emotional too about a people bonded by a strong commitment to shared values. For community truly to work, said Reinhold Niebuhr in *Moral Man and Immoral Society*, calculations of entitlement must be softened by a generous self-giving 'above and beyond the call of duty'.[36] We have to learn, says Charles Leadbeater, to value restraint as much as choice.

The role of the state is being redefined in the modern world. Governments are increasingly caught between the two millstones of pressure from global economic forces and demands from voters who want their insecurities and fears allayed. The assumption among politicians that there was nothing they could do may be one explanation of why confidence in politicians, throughout the world, is at an all-time low. It need not be so. Catholic Social Teaching offers pointers to lead us out of the technological determinism and fatalism which has dogged received wisdom in politics and sapped the will to do something about the humiliating situation of so many of our fellows throughout the world.

In the end we have to make an act of faith. Today the essential faultline lies not between those with religious belief and those for whom such a world view has no attraction. It is rather between optimism and pessimism, between those who instinctively have a sense of trust in the unfolding of human activity and those for whom, as some wag once put it, history is just one damned thing after another. We may speak in terms of the unfolding of a divine plan, with humankind playing a continuing role in the continuing creation. Or we may express some similar conviction in the secular language that each generation builds on the experience of its forebears. Either way, those who hold to the sense that there can be progress in human affairs must also hold to the conviction that there is fortuitous opportunity in the rapidly changing world we see around us, if only we can discern it. Catholic Social Teaching offers us the tools to do that.

Notes on Contributors

Michael Walsh edited (with Brian Davies) *Proclaiming Justice and Peace: One Hundred Years of Catholic Social Teaching*, Collins/CAFOD 1991. He is also the editor of the concise edition of *Butler's Lives of the Saints* and is the author of *Opus Dei*, Grafton Books 1989. A former Jesuit, he is the Librarian at Heythrop College, University of London.

Brian Davies edited (with Michael Walsh) *Proclaiming Justice and Peace: One Hundred Years of Catholic Social Teaching*, Collins/CAFOD 1991. He studied in Rome with the Society of Jesus and was the Head of Education at the Catholic aid and development agency CAFOD from 1980 to 1995.

Julian Filochowski, the director of CAFOD, has worked for the official aid agency of the Catholic Church in England and Wales since 1984. He lived and worked in Latin America for many years. He has contributed to *Reflections on Puebla*, CIIR 1979, and is the author of *Archbishop Romero: 10 Years On*, CIIR 1990.

Ian Linden, the director of the Catholic Institute for International Relations, is the author of *Church and Revolution in Rwanda*, Manchester University Press 1974; *The Catholic Church and the Struggle for Zimbabwe*, Longman 1980, and *Liberation Theology*, CIIR 1997.

Clifford Longley was for twenty years religious affairs editor of *The Times*, for which he was also chief leader writer. He now writes for *The Daily Telegraph* and *The Tablet* and is currently writing the official biography of the late Archbishop Derek Worlock. He was a consultant to the Catholic Bishops' Conference of England and Wales in producing *The Common Good and the Catholic Church's Social Teaching*, Gabriel Communications, Manchester 1996.

Julie Clague is a moral theologian. She teaches at St Mary's University College, London, and is currently engaged on research at Jesus College, Cambridge, on 'The Common Good'. She is a member of the editorial board of the journal *Political Theology*, published by Sheffield Academic Press, and is a former committee member of the Catholic Theological Association of Great Britain.

Paul Vallely writes on current social, ethical and political issues for *The Independent*. He has previously reported from thirty countries in the Third World. He is the Chair of the Catholic Institute for International Relations and of the fair trade organization Traidcraft Exchange. He has written a number of books on the Third World including *Bad Samaritans: First World Ethics and Third World Debt*, Orbis Books, Maryknoll, New York 1990.

Notes

Introduction

1. *Rerum Novarum*, 2.
2. *RN* 43.
3. *RN* 45.
4. *RN* 58.1.
5. Plato, *The Republic* 4.24OB. For a succinct discussion of the notion of the common good see the article by John Langan SJ in John Macquarrie and James Childress (eds), *A New Dictionary of Christian Ethics*, SCM Press 1986, p. 102.
6. Augustine, *City of God*, 19.21.
7. *Summa Theologica* I–II.90.2.
8. Ibid., II–II.64.2c.
9. *An Inquiry into the Original of our Ideas of Beauty and Virtue*, 1725, II.3.8.
10. *Principles of Morals and Legislation*, 1789, ch. 1.
11. *De Imitatione Christi*, I.19.4.
12. *Mater et Magistra*, 65.
13. *RN* 49.
14. *RN* 51.
15. *RN* 4.
16. *RN* 12.
17. *Quadragesimo Anno*, 79.
18. *QA* 88.
19. *Pacem in Terris*, 54.
20. *PT* 55.
21. *PT* 56.
22. *PT* 57.
23. *PT* 60.

24. *PT* 61.
25. *Gaudium et Spes*, 1.
26. *GS* 25.2.
27. *GS* 26.1.
28. *GS* 26.1.
29. *Octagesimo Adveniens*, 44.
30. *Populorum Progressio*, 58.
31. *OA* 26.
32. *OA* 34.
33. *Evangelii Nuntiandi*, 9.
34. *Justice in the World*, 6.
35. *OA* 4.
36. *JW* 40.
37. *Redemptor Hominis*, 16.7 .
38. *Sollicitudo Rei Socialis*, 36.
39. *SRS* 36.
40. *SRS* 37.
41. *SRS* 37.
42. *Centesimus Annus* 40.
43. *CA* 48.
44. *CA* 34.
45. *CA* 40.
46. *CA* 43.
47. *SRS* 38.
48. *SRS* 38.
49. *Evangelium Vitae*, 12.
50. *EV* 23.
51. *EV* 20.
52. Address to Pontifical Academy of Social Sciences, 25 April 1997, as reported in *Origins*, vol. 27, no. 3, 5 June 1997, in a translation from the French by *Osservatore Romano*.
53. Ibid.

1 Laying the Foundations

1. Cf., e.g., Charles Avila (ed), *Ownership: Early Christian Teaching*, Sheed and Ward 1983.

2. Cf., e.g., Justo L. González, *Faith and Wealth*, Harper and Row, San Francisco 1990.
3. Cf., e.g., J.-M Hornus, *It is not Lawful for Me to Fight*, Herald Press, Scottdale 1980.
4. Cf., e.g., John Gilchrist, *The Church and Economic Activity in the Middle Ages*, Macmillan 1969.
5. Edited by Judith Dwyer, Liturgical Press, Collegeville MN 1994.
6. It could be argued that de Vitoria's teaching on the relationship between states lies behind the 'trustee' system, or mandates, by which, in the aftermath of World War I, some parts of the world were put under the governance of far-off regimes.
7. And also, of course, from clerics, including Cardinal Manning of Westminster.
8. This is a criticism often made, cf., e.g., Graham Dawson, 'God's creation, wealth creation and the idle redistributor' in Digby Anderson (ed), *The Kindness that Kills*, SPCK 1984, pp. 13–20.
9. *Quadragesimo Anno*, 81–83.
10. See pp. 36–37 below
11. 'Octagesimo anno' in *Stimmen der Zeit*, vol. 187, 1971, pp. 289–96, ET in Charles E. Curran and Richard A. McCormick (eds), *Readings in Moral Theology No. 5: Official Catholic Social Teaching*, Paulist Press, New York/Mahwah 1986, pp. 60–68. The story of the writing of *Rerum Novarum* can be found in John Moloney, 'The Making of *Rerum Novarum*' in Paul Furlong and David Curtis (eds), *The Church Faces the Modern World*, The Earlsgate Press 1994, pp. 27–39; and the various recensions are discussed in Georges Jarlot, *Doctrine Pontificale et Histoire*, Gregorian University Press, Rome 1964, vol. I, pp. 202–25.
12. *QA* 94.
13. *QA* 95.
14. John A. Coleman, 'Development of Catholic Social Teaching' in Charles E. Curran and Richard A. McCormick (eds), *Readings in Moral Theology No. 5: Official Catholic Social Teaching*, Paulist Press, New York/Mahwah 1986, p. 183.
15. *Rerum Novarum* 33.
16. *RN* 48.1ff.
17. *RN* 5ff.

18. *QA* 79–80.
19. See pp. 38–39 below.
20. *QA* 120.
21. The same sort of considerations were at play when Leo XIII published *Rerum Novarum*. The rise of socialism in Germany had forced the Protestant monarchy to turn increasingly to the Centre Party, and Kaiser Wilhelm II, who succeeded to the throne in 1888, presented himself as something of a social reformer while obviously no radical. After all the battles of the *Kulturkampf*, it must have seemed appropriate to maintain the backing of the Centre Party for the Kaiser by rejecting the possibility that Catholics might associate themselves with the radicals as some Catholics were certainly tempted to do.
22. Coleman, art. cit., p. 184.
23. M.J. Walsh (ed), *Proclaiming Justice and Peace*, Collins 1991, pp. xxi–xxii. See also Georges Jarlot, op. cit.
24. *Mater et Magistra* 43.
25. *QA* 44ff.
26. Gordon Zahn, 'Social Movements and Catholic Social Thought' in John A. Coleman (ed), *One Hundred Years of Catholic Social Thought*, Orbis, Maryknoll, NY 1991, p. 52.
27. Brief *Quod aliquantum* of 10 March 1791, text to be found in Augustin Theiner (ed), *Documents Inédits relatifs aux Affaires Religieuses de la France* Paris, Frirmin Didot 1857, vol. I, pp. 32ff.
28. Cf. Richard C. Bayer, 'The Coherence of Catholic Social Thought' in *Horizons*, vol. 23, no. 1 (1996), pp. 72–85.
29. Washington DC, Georgetown UP 1991.
30. Coleman (ed), *One Hundred Years of Catholic Social Thought*, p. 4.
31. Coleman, art. cit., p.171.

2 Opening the Windows

1. Peter Hebblethwaite, *John XXIII: Pope of the Council*, Fount 1994.
2. *Mater et Magistra* 59–60.
3. *Centesimus Annus*, see pp. 107–13 below.
4. It is also the basis of the study and action programmes devised by

organizations like CAFOD.

5. *Pacem in Terris*, 11–27.
6. *PT* 36.
7. Margaret Thatcher, interview in *Woman's Own*, 26 October 1987.
8. *PT* 56.
9. *PT* 88.
10. *PT* 106.
11. *PT* 111–112.
12. *PT* 113.
13. *PT* 167.
14. John 14.27.
15. *Gaudium et Spes*, 1.
16. *GS* 62.6.
17. *GS* 69.
18. *GS* 74.
19. *GS* 76.

3 *Looking out to the World's Poor*

1. *Populorum Progressio*, 49. In what follows I am indebted to Donal Dorr's *Option for the Poor: 100 Years of Vatican Social Teaching*, Gill and Macmillan, Dublin 1983.
2. *PP* 7.
3. *PP* 9.
4. *PP* 57.
5. *PP* 58.
6. *PP* 59
7. *PP* 60–61.
8. *PP* 56–59.
9. *PP* 26.
10. *PP* 48–49; 76–77.
11. *PP* 54, 73.
12. *PP* 50–52; 60–61; 64.
13. *PP* 78.
14. *PP* 81–87.
15. *PP* 76–77; 83.
16. *PP* 49.

17. *PP* 30.
18. *PP* 31.
19. *PP* 29.
20. *PP* 32.
21. *PP* 48–49.
22. *PP* 61.
23. *PP* 50.
24. *PP* 78.
25. *PP* 79.
26. *PP* 15, 20, 65, 70.
27. *PP* 35.
28. *PP* 14–21.
29. The Millennium Jubilee is inspired by the Old Testament notion of Jubilee in which, every 50th year, debts would be cancelled, slaves freed and land returned to its original owners. Churches and other campaigners are pressing Western governments for a programme of debt forgiveness and reduction to ease the burden of Third World Debt which continues to cripple the development of many of the world's poorest peoples.
30. *Octagesima Adveniens*, 4.
31. See p. 47 above (ch. 2)
32. *OA* 9–12.
33. *OA* 13.1.
34. *OA* 13.2.
35. *OA* 14.1, 15.
36. *OA* 15.
37. *OA* 16.
38. *OA* 17.
39. *OA* 18.
40. *OA* 20.
41. *OA* 20.
42. *OA* 15.1.
43. *OA* 17.2.
44. *OA* 21.1.
45. *OA* 46.
46. *OA* 41.
47. *OA* 43.

48. *OA* 44.
49. *OA* 47.
50. *OA* 26.
51. He here follows what was said in *Pacem in Terris*, 159.
52. *OA* 4.
53. *OA* 23.
54. *OA* 23.
55. *OA* 14.
56. *OA* 50.
57. Joseph Cardinal Bernardin, *Common Ground*, National Pastoral Life Center, New York, 12 August 1996.
58. *Justice in the World*, 16.
59. *JW* 10.
60. *JW* 10.
61. *JW* 11.
62. *JW* 9.
63. *JW* 20.
64. *JW* 17.
65. *JW* 39.
66. *JW* 51, 52.
67. *JW* 40.
68. *JW* 47.
69. *JW* 47–48.
70. *JW* 30.
71. *JW* 31.
72. *JW* 35.
73. *JW* 36.
74. *JW* 6.
75. *Evangelii Nuntiandi*, 8.
76. *EN* 13.
77. Cf. *JW* 6.
78. *EN* 21.
79. *EN* 22.
80. *EN* 9.
81. *EN* 30.
82. *EN* 28.
83. *EN* 27.

84. *EN* 33.

85. *EN* 35.

86. *EN* 37.

87. *EN* 36.

88. *EN* 19.

89. *EN* 20.

90. *EN* 19.

91. But only following a rigorous process of questioning, purification or 'reconciliation', which can be traced through the two prior documents on liberation theology from the Sacred Congregation for the Doctrine of the Faith.

4   People before Profit

1. *Redemptor Hominis*, 14.

2. See p. 66 for Paul VI's first use of this term.

3. *RH* 16.7.

4. *Dives in Misericordia*, 11.

5. *RH* 15.1.

6. *DM* 11.4.

7. *DM* 11.3.

8. *RH* 15–16.

9. *RH* 16.9.

10. *RH* 17.6.

11. *DM* 12.2.

12. John Paul II, Pope, *The Acting Person, Analecta Husserliana, The Yearbook of Phenomenological Research*, vol. X, D. Reidel, Dordrecht, Holland 1979.

13. *Laborem Exercens*, 4–7.

14. *LE* 4–7.

15. *LE* 11–13.

16. *LE* 12–13.

17. Gregory Baum, *The Priority of Labour: A Commentary on Laborem Exercens, encyclical letter of Pope John Paul II*, Paulist Press, New York 1982.

18. *LE* 14.4.

19. *LE* 15.1.

20. *LE* 17.
21. See p. 101 below.
22. The eponymous hero of the celebrated satirical novel by the Czech writer Jaroslav Hasek. Schweik was a naive, honest, obliging, invariably incompetent figure who blundered through life and whose great achievement was merely to survive. *The Good Soldier Schweik*, tr. Cecil Parrott, Penguin 1974.

5   *Structures of Sin and the Free Market*

1. *Quadragesimo Anno,* 79–80.
2. *Sollicitudo Rei Socialis,* 38.
3. *SRS* 36.
4. *SRS* 36.
5. *SRS* 35.
6. *SRS* 37.
7. *SRS* 37.
8. *SRS* 37.
9. *SRS* 38.
10. *The Common Good and the Catholic Church's social teaching,* Catholic Bishops' Conference of England and Wales, Gabriel Communications, Manchester 1996, par. 78.
11. *QA* 88.
12. *Centesimus Annus,* 43.
13. *CA* 42.
14. *The Common Good,* par. 76–77.
15. See Paul Vallely on an option for the rich, 'A Lesson for Labour', *The Tablet,* 5 October 1996.
16. A development of the idea set out in *Justice in the World* that 'action on behalf of justice and participation in the transformation of the world fully appear to us as a constitutive dimension of the preaching of the Gospel, or, in other words, of the Church's mission for the redemption of the human race and its liberation from every oppressive situation' – see p. 76. Also Paul VI's insistence in *Evangelii Nuntiandi* that 'action for justice' and 'liberation for the poor' together with 'transformation of the world' are integral parts of the process of evangelization – see pp. 79–81.

17. *The Common Good*, par. 50.
18. *CA* 37.

6   *The Gospel of Life*

1. *Evangelium Vitae*, 13.
2. *EV* 91.
3. *EV* 58.
4. John Mahoney, *The Making Of Moral Theology: A Study of the Roman Catholic Tradition*, Clarendon Press 1987, p. 69.
5. Gary Lysaght, '*Evangelium Vitae*: The Moral Vision Of John Paul II Continued', p. 7; unpublished paper presented to the Association of Teachers of Moral Theology, Upholland, England, May 1996.
6. *EV* 96.
7. *EV* 21–22.
8. *EV* 23.
9. Book V, 19.
10. *EV* 95.
11. William Temple, *Christianity and Social Order*, Penguin 1942 as cited in John Atherton (ed), *Social Christianity: A Reader*, SPCK 1994, p. 95.
12. *EV* 12.
13. *EV* 90.
14. *EV* 57.
15. *EV* 27.
16. Cf. *EV* 19.
17. Cf. *EV* 69.
18. Cf. *EV* 13, 15.
19. Cf *EV* 12.
20. J.M. Keynes, *Liberalism and Labour*, 1926; as quoted in Ronald H. Preston, *Church and Society in the Late Twentieth Century*, SCM Press 1983, p. 47.
21. *EV* 23.
22. For a discussion of this, see J.F. Lyotard, *The Postmodern Condition: A Report on Knowledge*, Manchester University Press 1992 (first published in French 1979).

23. *EV* 19.

24. *EV* 98.

25. Richard Rorty, 'Truth and Freedom: A Reply to Thomas McCarthy' in Gene Outka and John P. Reeder (eds), *Prospects For A Common Morality*, Princeton University Press 1993, pp. 279–89, 280.

26. *EV* 19.

27. Brian Griffiths, *Morality and the Market Place: Christian Alternatives to Capitalism and Socialism*, Hodder and Stoughton 1982, pp. 71–72.

28. Cf. *Immortale Dei* (On The Christian Constitution Of States), 1885, 4, 36, 48; *Libertas Praestantissimum* (On The Nature Of Human Liberty), 1888, 44.

29. Cf. *Pacem in Terris*, 73; *Gaudium et Spes*, 75.

30. Cf. *Centesimus Annus*, 46.

31. Cf. *Immortale Dei*, 18, 24, 25, 31, 32, 37, 47.

32. *EV* 70.

33. *EV* 73.

34. *EV* 68.

35. Michael Novak, *The Spirit of Democratic Capitalism*, American Enterprise Institute/Simon and Schuster 1982, p. 334.

36. Ibid., p. 351.

37. *EV* 101.

38. Cf. *Libertas Praestantissimum*, 15, 16.

39. *EV* 20.

7   Into the Twenty-First Century

1. *Tertio Millennio Adveniente*, 25.

2. *TMA* 33.

3. *TMA* 33.

4. *TMA* 20.

5. *TMA* 23.

6. *TMA* 46.

7. In Asia 'the issue of the encounter of Christianity with ancient local cultures and religions is a pressing one' (*TMA* 38). The eve of the year 2000 will provide a great opportunity, especially in

view of the events of recent decades, for inter-religious dialogue. In this dialogue the Jews and the Muslims ought to have a pre-eminent place: 'In this regard attention is being given to finding ways of arranging historic meetings in places of exceptional symbolic importance like Bethlehem, Jerusalem and Mount Sinai' (*TMA* 53).

8. *TMA* 53.
9. *TMA* 36.
10. *TMA* 36.
11. *TMA* 47.
12. *Veritatis Splendor*, 113.2.
13. *TMA* 46.
14. *TMA* 51.
15. Address to Pontifical Academy of Social Sciences, 25 April 1997, as reported in *Origins*, vol. 27, no. 3, 5 June 1997, in a translation from the French by *Osservatore Romano*.
16. Ibid.
17. I am indebted to Clifford Longley for this analysis.
18. *The Common Good*, par. 34–35.
19. *TMA* 18.
20. Ian Markham, inaugural lecture for the Chair of Theology and Public Life at Liverpool Hope University, published in *Briefing*, Catholic Bishops' Conference of England and Wales, vol. 27, issue 7, 17 July 1997.
21. Ibid.
22. Ibid.
23. Ian Markham, *Plurality and Christianity Ethics*, CUP 1994.
24. Markham's lecture, art.cit., contains a study of the Vatican's recent dialogue with the advertising profession, of which Markham is highly critical.
25. Address to Pontifical Academy of Social Sciences, 25 April 1997, reported in *Origins*, op. cit.
26. Ibid.
27. John Lloyd, in *New Statesman*, 27 March 1997
28. Address to Pontifical Academy of Social Sciences, 25 April 1997, reported in *Origins*, op. cit.
29. Ibid.

30. In a lecture to a symposium of economists, political theorists and theologians at the Von Hügel Institute in Cambridge in January 1997, held to respond to the Catholic Bishops' document, *The Common Good*, op. cit.
31. John Gray, *After Social Democracy*, Demos 1997.
32. Francis Fukuyama, *Trust*, Penguin 1996.
33. George Soros, 'The Capitalist Threat', *Atlantic Monthly*, Boston, January 1997.

Epilogue

1. Geoff Mulgan, 'Connexity: how to live in a connected world', *Resurgence* magazine, no. 184, Sep/Oct 1997.
2. John Maynard Keynes, one of the twentieth century's leading economists, whose theories suggested that economic recession could be remedied by increasing public spending in a government sponsored policy of full employment. His most important work, *The General Theory of Employment, Interest and Money*, was published in 1936. *The Collected Writings of John Maynard Keynes* are published in 29 volumes by the Royal Economic Society, London 1971–79.
3. John Gray, *After Social Democracy*, Demos 1997, p. 11.
4. Jonathan Sacks, *Faith in the Future*, Darton, Longman and Todd 1995, pp. 62–68.
5. *Evangelium Vitae*, 12.
6. Gray, op. cit., pp. 19, 35.
7. See note 2 above.
8. Gray, op cit., p. 19.
9. Sacks, op. cit.
10. Alasdair MacIntyre, *After Virtue: A Study in Moral Theory*, 2nd edn, University of Notre Dame Press 1984. See also his *Secularization and Moral Change*, OUP 1967, pp. 24, 25.
11. Sacks, op. cit.
12. Michael Walzer, *Spheres of Justice*, Blackwell 1983, quoted in the essay by Frank Turner in Peter Askonas and Stephen F. Frowen (eds), *Welfare and Values*, Macmillan 1997.
13. Sacks, op. cit.

14. See Mulgan's book *Connexity: how to live in a connected world*, Chatto 1998. Demos is an independent group of social scientists, political philosophers, business people and journalists which publishes books, papers and a quarterly journal offering radical solutions to long-term problems.

15. Geoff Mulgan, 'Connexity: how to live in a connected world', *Resurgence* magazine, no. 184, Sep/Oct 1997.

16. Ibid.

17. Charles Leadbeater, *Civic Spirit: The Bid Idea for a New Political Era*, Demos 1997, p. 5.

18. New Year Message, *The Guardian*, 1 January 1997.

19. *Laborem Exercens*, 6.

20. Traidcraft Exchange, Kingsway, Gateshead, NE11 0NE. New Economics Foundation, Vine Court, 112–116 Whitechapel Road, London E1 1JE.

21. In response to judgments made by external monitoring from scrutineering groups like Ethical Consumer which produces a regular magazine dedicated to the process. Ethical Consumer, Unit 21, 41 Old Birley St, Manchester M15 5RF.

22. A coalition of leading UK development organizations – including CAFOD, the Catholic Institute for International Relations (CIIR), Christian Aid, Consumer International, the Fairtrade Foundation, the New Economics Foundation, Oxfam and the World Development Movement – was formed in March 1997 to tighten up on the monitoring and verification of the Codes of Conduct of leading companies.

23. As defined by the Highly Indebted Poor Countries initiative of the IMF/World Bank.

24. Excluding oil. *Global economic prospects and the developing countries*, World Bank, Washington 1993.

25. Kevin Watkins, *Globalisation and liberalisation: the implications for poverty, distribution and inequality*, internal Oxfam report 1997.

26. Peter Selby, *Grace and Mortgage*, Darton, Longman and Todd 1998.

27. James Tobin, a Nobel-Prize-winning economist, proposed in 1978 that a small tax (as little as one quarter of one per cent) should be levied by all major countries on all foreign exchange

transactions. This rate would be low enough not to have a significant effect on longer term investment but it would cut into the yields of speculators moving massive amounts of currency around the globe as they seek to profit from minute differentials in currency fluctuations.

28. See 'Floating the Tobin Tax', *The Economist*, 13 July 1996. But there seems no reason why implementation of the Tobin Tax could not be made a prerequisite for membership in the International Monetary Fund and the World Bank, were there the political will to do so.

29. R. H. Tawney, *Religion and the Rise of Capitalism*, 1922; Penguin 1972.

30. Address to Pontifical Academy of Social Sciences, reported in *Origins*, op. cit.

31. *Tertio Millennio Adveniente*, 18.

32. On this see Martyn Percy, *Intimate Affairs: sexuality and spirituality in perspective*, Darton, Longman and Todd 1997, who shows that marriage commonly followed sex in England during the fifteenth and sixteenth centuries.

33. In an interview with the author: Paul Vallely, 'No Time Wasters Please', *Independent Saturday Magazine*, 28 March 1998.

34. Sacks, op. cit.

35. Leadbeater, op. cit.

36. Reinhold Niebuhr, *Moral Man and Immoral Society*, SCM Press 1963.

Index